RESURRECTION MESSAGES

RESURRECTION MESSAGES

by

John M. Gordon

BAKER BOOK HOUSE
Grand Rapids, Michigan

Library of Congress Catalog Card
Number 64–8348

ISBN: 0–8010–3657–7

Third printing, November 1978

PHOTOLITHOPRINTED BY CUSHING - MALLOY, INC.
ANN ARBOR, MICHIGAN, UNITED STATES OF AMERICA
1978

To the memory of my father, worthy
of emulation as a translucent preacher
and a faithful Christian man.

Foreword

The first apostles as heralds of the Resurrection were not only proclaiming it as a fact, "they were living in it as in a new country" (James S. Stewart, *A Faith to Proclaim*, Hodder and Stoughton, 1953, p. 109). The author of these resurrection messages does the same thing. "With the map of (this) brand new country in his hand" he lives and moves and has his being "in gospel territory."

John Gordon often alliterates the key-words of his sermons. There are three key-words, each starting with the letter "c," which give us a clue to the very depth of his resurrection messages. The three words are "Conviction," "Commitment" and "Confession."

Conviction. Paul in his first epistle reminded the Thessalonians: the gospel he proclaimed came to them "not only in word, but also in power and in the Holy Spirit"; however, he hastened to add: "and with full conviction." John Gordon proclaims the crucified and risen Lord with full conviction.

Commitment. The central theme of the Christian message and our basic belief in it can lay hold of us only through our ever fresh commitments to Him who died for us all, yet who as our risen Lord offers to us "a life-transforming companionship" with Him. John Gordon's way to a full conviction of the Resurrection was (and still is) a step by step commitment. And that is exactly what makes it so sincere and convincing.

Confession is the third key-word that will lead us to an even deeper understanding and the fullest possible appraisal of these resurrection messages; confession, not only in the sense of oral proclamation from elevated pulpits; nor just in the sense of the affirmation of faith done in unison by a worshiping congregation; but first of all and above everything else, in the sense of one's whole-life-involvement, as a constant struggle to live for Christ and for others for His sake. Confession, says Gordon, means living victoriously and vicariously and doing this always happily. It means learning and manifesting in our every days and every ways that "holiness is happiness": "Christ is risen, therefore any one of us can serve successfully" and happily.

My wife and I have listened quite often to John Gordon's sermons as they were delivered from his Lancaster pulpit. But whether we heard him preach the Word, or observed his shining face at the church door after the delivery of one of his resurrection messages; whether we received his pastoral call in our home or his consolation at the hospital bed; whether he served our family as a "liturgist" or as a personal counselor, I was compelled to recall again and again one of the marginal notes of the four hundred year old Second Helvetic Confession: "The proclamation of the Word of God *is* the Word of God" *(praedicatio Verbi Dei est Verbum Dei)*. The Word fitly spoken and appropriately spelled out in one's own life alone constitutes the faithful soldier of the Jesus Christ.

It was a daring act for John Gordon to publish a book that contains nothing else but resurrection sermons. But we who know him have our good reasons to assure him, he was the right man to dare such a thing: not only because his sermons represent the rich gamut of maturing Christian experience, and his approach to his listeners (and readers) that of a surgeon whose knife not only cuts but also heals; nor simply because the language is so clear, direct and picturesque that one can not help but be attracted by it; but above all this because he himself is a man of conviction, a man of commitment and a man of confession.

Bela Vassady
Professor of Systematic Theology
Lancaster Theological Seminary
Lancaster, Pennsylvania
Vienna, August 31, 1964

Contents

1. The Heart of the Gospel (I Corinthians 15:1-4) .. 13

2. Three Who Believed (John 20:29) 27

3. Either/Or (Matthew 28:5, 6) 39

4. Our Recognition of His Presence (Luke 24:32) .. 51

5. Beyond Bewilderment (Mark 16:6, 7) 63

6. Living in the Light of Easter (John 21:14) 75

7. Something Wonderful — Something Terrible —
   Something Dreamed About — and Something
   Seen (Luke 24:36-48) 89

8. The Body That Shall Be (I Corinthians 15:35) ...101

9. The Whereabouts of Our Risen Lord (Acts 1:9) ..115

10. Two Roads to Christian Certitude (John 29:29) ..127

Chapter I

The Heart of the Gospel

"Now I would remind you, brethren, in what terms I preached to you the gospel, which you received, in which you stand, by which you are saved, if you hold it fast — unless you believed in vain. For I delivered to you as of first importance what I also received, that Christ died for our sins in accordance with the scriptures, that he was buried, that he was raised on the third day in accordance with the scriptures . . . ." — I Corinthians 15:1-4

Two quite different images come to mind when the word "heart" is used. We may think *sentimentally*, in love lyric style, of a sweet, symmetrical Valentine-shaped something that feels good when one's beloved smiles, and aches when she pouts. Or one may think *surgically*, his imagination probing deep into the human chest cavity to where a raw, red muscle thumps and pumps to circulate the warm river which keeps our whole marvelous body alive.

One can conceive of "The Heart of the Gospel" either sentimentally or surgically. It is sometimes little more than a neat formula to be framed and hung as a wall motto, or to be harmonized pleasantly in a gospel chorus. Or we may depend upon it as a vital organ in the body of Christian truth, throbbing with existential significance.

To return for a moment to the physical heart, I must confess to knowing very little about it except what I have read in popular magazines. When one of our modern day presidents was stricken, the American people became heart-specialists of sorts — so detailed was press treatment of the subject. We learned something of the complexity of its structure. Perhaps we had never realized that it is not a single but a double pumping mechanism, having its right side occupied constantly with the process of getting blood to and from the lungs for purposes of purification, and its left section busy circulating the blood around through the rest of the body for its nourishment.

This verbal "cardioscope" may help us to see the shape of what we have called the Heart of the Gospel and how it is expressed in the two verses which comprise our text. The good news about Jesus Christ has two sides to it. He died for our sins according to the Scriptures, and He rose again the third day according to the Scriptures. So Paul's twin affirmations give us the pattern for our sermon.

1. *"Christ died for our sins according to the Scriptures."*

His death was *"for our sins."* This is to say that He did not perish as a martyr but offered Himself as an atoning sacrifice. He was the divinely appointed Lamb to be offered, according to the precedent in the Book of Moses, as a substitute for sinners.

Some so-called liberal theologians react violently against this New Testament doctrine. They use adjectives like "barbaric" and "sadistic," and expressions like "slaughter-house religion," to describe it. They find the thought of someone having to die for them repulsive and immoral. Men with famous names in the field of religion have talked that way, and others express their displeasure by ignoring the subject altogether in their sermons and, one infers, in their personal reading as well.

I find myself wondering whether this tendency to become nauseated by the idea of Christ's death being necessary to save sinners may not be like the proverbial Victorian attitude toward sex! There is a prudery which feels sick when sex is mentioned. Sexuality can manifest itself in ways that are impure, unnatural and brutal. Yet prudery itself is unwholesome. It can become a mental illness.

By the same token we may admit that there have been perversions of man's religious instinct which have led him into gross cruelty or a hysterical delight in human or animal suffering. Beautiful maidens have been tossed into volcanoes, and tiny babies laid in the red hot laps of grinning idols, to propitiate the gods or to guarantee the success of generals. But to compare Christ's death on His cross to these acts is like bringing a pornographic picture book to a wedding and telling the bride and groom that this is what marriage is about. To say the least, it betrays a very limited range of comprehension!

Underneath all of the perversions of sacred sacrificial bloodshed lies a true, God-given instinct that the wages of sin is death, and that without shedding of blood there is no remission of sins.

Christ's death for our sins was *according to the Scriptures*. "The Old Testament is the New concealed; the New Testament is the Old revealed." Hints of the necessity of the cross are found by the Christian as far back in the Bible as the book of Genesis. Devout commentators see a hazy foreshadowing of it in Genesis 3:15 where the bruising of the serpent's head is seen to involve the wounding of a representative Man. Others sense a call for costly sacrifice, involving a slain animal, in God's favorable response to Abel's offering and His lack of respect for Cain's surplus vegetables. The cost requirement is spelled out in great detail for tabernacle offerings by the law of Moses. It was imported into Palestine with the Ark of the Covenant and became the central ceremony at the Temple in Jerusalem. And if we take the lead of the New Testament church in its interpretation of the Jewish Scriptures, the Suffering Servant of Isaiah's prophecy can be none other than Jesus Christ glimpsed from afar. He is a strange and tragic figure not yet clearly identified by whoever penned the passage. But the principle of vicarious suffering and death is explicit:

"The Lord hath laid on him the iniquity of us all!"

When we get to the New Testament itself, we find Jesus early trying to forewarn his followers that His death lies ahead, and that it will be a purposeful dying which He must undergo in order to fulfil His ministry. They had had hints from John the Baptist, their earlier teacher, that Jesus was the "Lamb of God." If the title did not register, there is reason to suppose that it was not because the connotation was foreign to them, but because every ounce of their Jewish patriotism was resisting the proposal that the Messiah would have to die. Even John, who coined the phrase, was troubled when it began to appear that the One who he thought should be sinking His axe into the roots of a rotting society might Himself get the axe instead. But as He was able, Jesus more and more took His friends into His confidence, attempting to show them not just that He must die, but why. The Last Supper was the final object lesson before the awful thing itself.

"Take, eat. This is my body, broken for you; my blood for the remission of sins. . . ."

Only after the resurrection and the forty days of intensive instruction, did the disciples really dare to discuss the matter out loud. And only then were they prepared to understand its implications. Now it became for them the heart of their gospel (or rather the first half of its heart!). The letters of Paul and the others are permeated with the gratitude each writer felt because his Master by dying for him had become his Savior. Paul was determined never to preach a sermon without its being controlled by the recollection of Jesus Christ and Him crucified.

> "Scarcely for a righteous man would one die; yet peradventure for a good man some would even dare to die. But God commendeth His love toward us, in that, while we were yet sinners, Christ died for us!"

Here is the answer to man's instinctive longing for the cleansing of his conscience. Here is why the murder of the world's best man and greatest teacher is good news. For *good news* is what the word "gospel" means in literal English. The first half of the heart of the gospel is the story of purification, just as it is with the right side of the heart that beats within you.

For some people, the characteristic Scripture stress on sin sounds like anything but good news. "Let's hear more about the nobility of man, about his achievements over the centuries, about his exciting prospects in the decades just ahead! Why this morbid preoccupation with man's faults? Give him time and he will grow out of them." One might as well plead for a candy valentine heart in the man's chest as for a gospel which would consist of telling folks how nice they are! Or, to be a little less fanciful, why is there not *one* interior pump for circulating the bloodstream? Let us omit the purification cycle! The thought has the merit of simplicity, and to implement it would probably solve all our problems for we would presently be dead. But our Creator knew better what we needed, and so, instead of smothering us with body sewage, our heart works night and day with its one side to keep its output pure. Thanks be to Thee, O Lord!

And thank God too for refusing to ignore sin's poison in our lives. Not all preaching about the subject is wholesome, and no doubt certain of the objections churchgoers raise are deserving of our sympathy. Preachers sometimes flog their congregations because of their own inner frustations, just as there are husbands who come home from work and vent their weariness or their exasperation about the boss by snarling at their wives and browbeating their children. "One should never preach on Hell except with tears," Charles Spurgeon once remarked, and sin ought to be dealt with in church, or in the counseling room, or wherever it is encountered by the Christian, in accordance with the way God's Word confronts it. Jesus makes the method most clear. He hated sin, but loved the sinner. He was tough with the defiant, but tender with the contrite. He dealt with the penitent always in a context of forgiveness, and He could say with authority, "Thy sins be forgiven thee!" because He was in perfect touch with the will of the Father into whose hands He would soon commend His spirit while dying on an atoning cross.

"He died that we might be forgiven; He died to make us good:
That we might go at last to heaven, saved by His precious blood."

You see, the gospel focuses on man's sin in order that man may know the secret of overcoming it. Christ died not just to make us sin-conscious but to make us sin conquerors! And when one who has taken Him as Savior speaks of sin, it should never be with the expression or the tone of someone describing his own or another's incurable illness. The Christian should think and talk like a cured man, or at least like one who is well on the road to recovery! For the believer, sin is something which once had the upper hand but now is under control. It may continue to threaten, but the specific remedy is known. "Sin hath no more dominion over you." "We are debtors not to the flesh to live after the flesh." "If we confess our sins, He is faithful and just to forgive us our sins, and to cleanse us from all unrighteousness." This is how the New Testament takes account of sin.

How many of us are living in gospel territory as far as our awareness of sin and its cure are concerned? Some people we know who make no Christian profession whatever are living frankly settled as citizens of Satan's realm, doomed and at least externally delighted. Other who know better are convicted of their need of a Savior and of talking-back to temptation, but they are not too hopeful of living at much more than what the hymn-writer calls "this poor dying rate." Faintly aware that Jesus preached forgiveness, vaguely conscious that some Christians live victoriously, their only real hope of healing lies beyond the grave. Meanwhile they do "the best they can" which is not much more than dutiful performance of religious routines.

I had a parishioner once whom penicillin could have saved, the physician said. It was during the early stages of that drug's development. Doctor and patient knew there was such an antibiotic. But it was inaccessible, however, so she and her physician simply resigned themselves to her dying; and die she did. Here is a parable for us in matters spiritual. That millions in far away lands regard the struggle with acknowledged sin as hopeless is a familiar theme of returned missionaries, and we are motivated to get the hope-full gospel out where they can hear it. But what is far more strange and tragic is the multitude under the very eaves of the churches, in a country where the

Word has had free course for generations, who do not seem to grasp that Jesus died for them.

This mysterious ability of ours to hear the gospel and not to listen is not peculiar to our time. Jesus took account of it too. He saw it as a complication of the basic sinfulness of man. It is as if a mental illness were superimposed upon an organic disease so that a man will not reach out for the medical attention which could save him. Our Lord used a more elementary illustration in His parable of the soils. Much seed falls on stony, packed, or thorn-infested ground. "He came unto his own, and his own received him not." Some seed finds good soil, and "As many as received him, to them gave he power to become children of God."

Charles Simeon, the English University Preacher, has the following entry in his journal:

> "In Passion Week as I was reading Bishop Wilson on the Lord's Supper, I met with an expression to this effect — 'That the Jews knew what they did when they transferred their sin to the head of their offering.' The thought came into my mind, 'What, may I transfer all my guilt to another? Has God provided an Offering for me that I may lay my sins on His head? Then God willing, I will not bear them on my own soul one moment longer.' Accordingly I sought to lay my sins on the sacred head of Jesus, and on Wednesday I began to have a hope of mercy; on Thursday that hope increased. On Friday and Saturday it became more strong; and on Sunday morning — Easter Day, April 4th, I awoke early with these words upon my heart and lips, — *Jesus Christ is Risen Today, Hallelujah! Hallelujah!* From that hour peace flowed in rich abundance into my soul."

"Christ died for our sins according to the Scriptures."

2. *"And He rose again the third day according to the Scriptures."*

The progress of Charles Simeon's life-changing Holy

Week pilgrimage is logical in its direction. It starts at the foot of the cross and leads past the empty tomb on into the peaceful, powerful Christian living which in Simeon's case influenced thousands of college students for God. So strong was his impact on Cambridge University that at his death the bells of all the colleges were tolled, an honor usually reserved for only the most eminent Britons.

A similar logic informs the whole New Testament, and defies the attempts of faithless men to close the life of Jesus with His crucifixion. His death and resurrection are twin truths — Siamese twins. They are two sides of the same heart. In our text Paul has them together where they belong. They are of the same quality historically. We are not to try to make Christian doctrine more digestible or palatable to the mind of modern man by proposing that the death was actual but the resurrection "ideal"; that the one was historical and the other mythological. Such a theory is not modern at all. It is as old as the book of Acts, and it is utterly foreign to the message of the gospel. It is fatal to the faith.

So Paul lists the names of those who saw the Lord. They are honorable, sensible men. Their word is their bond.

Furthermore, again, Christ's rising was according to the Scriptures. It was no freak. It was foreshadowed in the Bible of the first century Jews, our Old Testament.

I must confess to having been troubled at this point. Jesus, we are told, took his disciples back into their Scriptures and showed that it was necessary according to Moses and all the prophets for the Messiah "to have suffered . . . and to enter into his glory." Yet, if you read the Old Testament looking for prophecies of the resurrection of Jesus, you may be disappointed, for they are not of the obvious, explicit variety. Does this mean that they had inspired writings we know nothing about? Hardly. I believe, rather, that what He would be pointing out to them would be that His victory at Easter was not to be thought of as an isolated happening once in time, but as the outcropping of a great organizing principle underlying all of life and history. Here at the empty tomb God had bared His arm (and His heart) in a "Moment of Truth." Here in the person of His Son He had let us behold His glory, and by the afterglow the whole universe was illumined.

Resurrection is everywhere anticipated in the Old Testament. That's the point. It is like $E=MC^2$ in nature — long concealed, spelled out even now only in a limited literature, nowhere obtrusive but operative everywhere. The program of life-from-death, of victory rising out of defeat, is God's consistent way of working. Whether you have in view the current international crisis or the adventures of the Children of Israel; whether you wrestle with the problems of the book of Job or stand beside the open grave of someone dear to you and wonder why he had to go so soon — persistent questions about meanings will raise themselves. Into these and all the other big, deep doubts which plague us, the resurrection fits like a master key. Anywhere you look in the Bible from the standpoint of men B.C., you will find delicate locks on tantalizing doors which are themselves witnesses to a Creator who holds a key. But now He no longer withholds that key. He shares it. "That which we have seen and heard declare we unto you, and truly our fellowship is with the Father and with His Son Jesus Christ." So the New Testament gospel narrative begins, and ushers in A.D.

Then here is the second side of the gospel's heart. And it too is very good news. Still, strangely, an unconverted man (Paul calls him the "natural man") does not relish the doctrine of Christ's resurrection any more than His atoning death for sinners. I should like to think that such resistance is not entirely wickedness. Some of it may be misinformation: the harboring of misleading mental images. If the word resurrection suggests, for instance, the regathering, à la trick photography, of each of the components of this very body from every place where oxidation has dispersed them, it poses some sticky problems. If resurrection means a popping up from coffins underground such as literalistic old time artists used to love to paint, no wonder modern man finds the thought grotesque. But these objections have little relationship to what the Bible means, and they sound as often as not like mere excuses.

More likely the uneasiness of moderns is the same as it has always been. The resurrection concept, claimed for Jesus then, or projected for ourselves later on, is just too carnal for comfort! The thought of immortality for the soul is dreamlike, and dreams, when recognized as such, no longer disturb us. But the doctrine which requires us to show up for Judgment day as whole persons, no wraiths, makes death more serious than mere falling off to sleep. It drives home the crucial quality of the use we make of our bodies here and now. "For we must all appear before the judgment seat of Christ; that every one may receive the things done in his body, according to what he hath done, whether it be good or bad." Paul puts the fear of God into pagan hearts with that sort of language! No wonder that self-indulgent men do not want to hear it. The Greek idea of immortality is man-centered. It would offer escape from responsibility, and psychic bliss like that which some seek in opiates. Resurrection is God-centered in its implications. Why expect the unbeliever or lukewarm Christian to covet that kind of a situation, so foreign to his idea of fun?

For the believer, though, who knows forgiveness and has tasted initial victories over sin, the Easter message is fraught with prospects both joyful and hopeful.

In the remainder of this explanatory chapter, Paul deals first with history and the bearing of the gospel on its outcome. For paganism in Paul's time, history was conceived as cyclic. For the Christian, he indicates, it is no longer a merry-go-round (or misery-go-round, some would call it) but a guided march toward a Goal. And what a Goal! You will have to read the entire New Testament to get the full picture. Old Testament prophecy will help too. "Eye hath not seen; nor ear heard; neither have entered into the heart of man" what God has in store for His pilgrim people!

Next Paul proceeds to deal with the destiny of the individual lover of Jesus. There are brief, impressionistic word pictures of the body each of us will inhabit. I am excited at the prospects, and suspect that you are too if you have considered them. We are to have something essentially similar to Christ's glorious resurrection physique. Frankly, I was not nearly so much interested thirty years or so ago when I imagined, as most young men do, that I already had a glorious body and that it could do practically anything I wanted to do. The reason was that my wants were youthful ones, narrow in range and short on sense.

I am older now, and there are so many more things I would like to accomplish with my body than would have interested me, way back then! To play the piano would be one, and to design a bridge; to build a house from footings to final nail; to understand chemistry and thereby perhaps discover some brand new substances to benefit mankind; to read all of the world's great literature (without glasses!); to run a prosperous farm; to explore outer space, and open new frontiers. Now you make a list!

The more a person lives and learns, the more he comes to realize that this body of his, wonderfully designed and efficient as it is, is nonetheless what Paul calls it in Philippians 3:21. ("This vile body," the King James Version quotes him as saying, but that is a poor translation. "This *humiliating* body" renders it better.) Instead of obeying my spirit, my physical machinery can not help hampering it. My energies lumber along behind my adventurous imagination. From observation, and some beginning experience too, I know that in a few brief years this frame of mine will start to creak and totter and collapse. Yours will, too. You are not so very much younger yourself!

If somewhere on good authority I could learn of the possibility of exchanging it for a new model, more powerful and gorgeous in contrast to the old one than your new Cadillac compared with my grandson's kiddie-car. . . . Well, on the best of Authority we have it that, as we have identified ourselves with Jesus in His dying for us on the cross, so we shall be "with him in the likeness of his resurrection!"

* * *

We have two choices, now that we have listened to the gospel. One is to react as sensible persons react to folk tales — of flying carpets and fairy godmothers, of Hercules, or Paul Bunyan, or of Superman. We can muse, "Wouldn't it be great if only true!" and let it go at that.

Some professing Christians thus estimate their Bibles. They might be justified in this if evidence kept pouring in that the Scriptures are full of holes historically, logically, and scientifically — a collection of antiquated nonsense. The remarkable fact, however, is that as archaeologists dig, and critics sift, and ancient manuscripts turn up in caves, and as Christians test the promises of Holy Writ in all kinds of everyday situations, the evidence turns out to be consistently on the side of the trustworthiness of what we call God's Word.

So the other choice is to believe! The invitation of the Good News Reporters is to do just this. Here is Paul's motive for laying open to our view the Heart of the Gospel which he preaches, which many of us present have received as God's truth, and in which we have taken our stand. If you too will take your stand with us, believing that Christ died for your sins according to the Scriptures, and that He rose again the third day according to the Scriptures, you will be saved from sin and for eternity. You will have reason to be

> "stedfast, unmovable, always abounding in the work of the Lord, forasmuch as you know that your labor is not in vain in the Lord."

Chapter II

Three Who Believed

"Jesus said to him 'Have you believed because you have seen me? Blessed are those who have not seen and yet believe.'" — John 20:29

John's report of what happened the first Easter day is quite different from what the other Gospel writers tell us. Not contradictory, but different. There is a fundamental agreement in all four accounts of what took place. But there is this notable contrast: that while Matthew, Mark, and Luke deal largely with events, John concentrates on persons.

His twentieth chapter, for example, can be seen as dividing into three biographical incidents, each with a particular individual shown arriving at assurance that Jesus had indeed risen from the dead. Each of the three may be thought of as representing a different type of person. One of them, perhaps, is "just like you." More likely still, each of them stands for one of the several moods or personality strands in any one of us.

The three who believed include first the Apostle John himself, although, as is his practice, he does not mention his own name. The second is Mary Magdalene, and the third Doubting Thomas. Let us not only identify them but *identify with* them, for it is by putting ourselves imaginatively in the stead of the various Bible characters that we can learn what God has to say to us through each. For example:

1. *JOHN Suggests the Approach of the Logical Mind*

John seems to have been the philosopher of the disciple company. That he came from a cultured Jewish family is indicated in the New Testament by certain literary clues, and is confirmed by ancient tradition. His partnership with brothers and father in a productive Galilean fishing operation does not need to conflict with such an assumption. In Biblical Palestine, as in "The Flowering of New England," men wise in the classics knew how to work with their hands. And if, as there is no convincing reason to doubt, John was the source of the Gospel which bears his name, the style and subject matter of his writing bear out the church's recollection that he was a competent intellectual, quite at home with the writings of the Greeks as well as with the prophets of Israel. An ancient symbol of this gospel writer was a soaring eagle, suggesting the imagination of a poet and the sharp eye of a scientist.

We are told that John looked at the contents of the deserted tomb, "and believed." What he saw, as his eyes became accustomed to the semi-darkness, was the strange basis, apparently, for his belief in the resurrection of his Lord. He saw, and Peter confirmed it, "the linen cloths lying, and the napkin, which had been on Jesus' head, not lying with the linen cloths but rolled up in a place by itself."

Such detail may sound quite irrelevant unless we can visualize the mode in which respected people of the time were buried. They were bound around and around with bandages until encased in a linen cocoon. Then the head was wrapped separately in a linen napkin, and the corpse so swaddled was laid out on the slab prepared for it. Are you able to picture the body of Jesus thus treated? And can you now look with John's eyes at the place where Nicodemus and Joseph of Arimathea had reverently laid him? There are the linen cloths, still wrapped in loops. There is the napkin, neatly folded where Jesus' head had been. *But the body is gone!* The grave clothes undisturbed meant only one thing to John's probing mind. Jesus had moved out of his linen strait-jacket without any unwinding or breaking of the fabric. This was not, as had been the case with Lazarus, earlier, a miraculous resuscitation — wonderful as that would have been. It was not a reanimation, that is, of a body that had ceased to breathe and begun to deteriorate. Rather, here was evidence of *transmutation:* a change of material as distinct as the turning of water into vapor or of matter into energy!

I cannot help connecting this glimpse of John, staring at the graveclothes, with another scene I can recall reading about some years ago. Albert Einstein is lying on his back on the deck of a vessel steaming through the Mediterranean Sea, looking up into the blue depths above, when suddenly he "sees" his concept of matter which is to revolutionize science and let into human life the practical utilization of atomic energy with all its potency for good or ill. Or one thinks of Madame Curie's wide-eyed recognition that the chunk of coarse pitchblende in her hand holds the secret of available radium. Three Greek words for "seeing" follow one another in quick succession in the Bible passage now before us: John *blepei* (glanced); Peter *theorei* (stared); then John went in and *eide* (perceived or "saw into").

John doubtless knew the philosophical Greek theory of immortality — that the soul of man departed from the body at death, leaving the corpse to rot and return to dust. But here was evidence of something more than the soul's capacity to escape and live on. Here was *resurrection* — new body for old. Here were strange new powers for defying ordinary limitations of time and space and for transcending material barriers. Here was initial corroboration for John that when Jesus would that same evening come into the room where the disciples were to be gathered, He would enter in spite of locked doors, but He would be no ghost. Each encounter with the risen Christ would be reminding them of what John here realized. Jesus was physically alive in a new dimension. His body now was the perfect servant of His spirit, as indeed ours too shall be some day for His sake and at His command.

Men had no adequate scientific vocabulary in Jesus' time to describe the relationship between matter and energy. Witnesses like Paul and John who voiced their resurrection faith in preaching and writing were forced to resort to much simpler analogies — the seed is only fulfilled in the plant; flesh of fish differs from that of animals; stars vary in their "glory" (a most expressive ancient word to describe radiant energy). Jesus had to hint at the breathtaking meaning of what had happened, not alone by coming through barred doors, but also by eating broiled fish in their presence. This body was different, but it was definite too. "I am no ghost; it is I myself!"

How Paul would have reveled in the analogies to be drawn from today's physics. We yawn now at marvels which make the romancing of Jules Verne or of the unknown author of Arabian Nights seem tame indeed. How delighted John would have been could he have drawn on twentieth century terminology to illustrate what the empty grave cloths meant. But he grasped enough of their import to be himself an example of the great truth that the more a person alerts his intellect, the more sound sense the resurrection gospel makes. The more we learn about the universe, our physical home, the more we may expect to feel at home intellectually and spiritually in the New Testament.

John, looking into the empty sepulchre and perceiving what had occurred, represents man's inquiring mind as it suddenly comes to see that the answer to its deepest questions is in Christ, crucified and risen. The Word made flesh to dwell among us is also the latest, surest word concerning the nature of the body that shall be. This is the legitimate inference of the logical mind as it looks into the evacuated tomb.

2. *MARY MAGDALENE Represents the Insight of the Hungry Heart*

She was a woman, and a very feminine one at that. She had been too much the female in the past, for she had had a "past" during which her sex had been the most noticeable thing about her. A new creature now, but still a woman, here she is weeping as women will when their emotions are stirred. She is turning from the tomb, not having noticed the grave clothes. They would only have baffled her if she had. Her snap-judgment was that someone had stolen the body of her Lord. Others, more calculating, would propose the same theory in time to come as a way of explaining away Christ's triumph. As a theory it will not stand the test of logic, but for Mary it was

no theory — only a guess. And women do not need to
be long on logic. They have intuition! Sometimes it works
well, and again not. Blinded by her tears, and perhaps
also by His deliberate disguise, she supposed that He was
the gardener. Her intuition was a bit off beam.

No, this is not trying to be facetious. I am just trying
to echo the sort of thing the more level-headed male
disciples would be saying a little later when some of the
women would be returning from the sepulchre to report
a vision of angels who announced that Jesus was alive.
You can almost hear the men scoff. "You girls are always
seeing and hearing what you want to see and hear.
'Angels?' More likely the brush of bats' wings, or owls
heading home to roost. 'Men in white?' Wisps of early
morning fog, perhaps!"

But the women are not to be so lightly dismissed. We
men do well not to forget that they were last at the cross
and the first at the tomb. And more than once in Christian
history since, it has been a woman who has kept the flame
of the faith burning. God surely knew what he was doing
when he made us male and female. If woman's intuition
has its limitations, so, too, does man's intellect. Mary did
at first mistake Jesus for the gardener, but when He spoke
her name — "Mary!" — she knew without looking who it
was. "Rabboni!" she replied, "Dear, dear Master!"

Thank God for Mary, and for her intuitions. Thank God
for the reasons of the heart, as well as of the head. Logic
has its limits. And while selfish love can be blind, true
love is deeply discerning. Besides, let us not exaggerate
the difference, or settle it on the separate sexes. Every
normal human is both head and heart, intellect and
instinct. The gospel places these case histories in their
proper order. John was a "brain" who saw that there are
tremendous theological implications in the resurrection.

But to *see God,* Jesus clearly told us, a man (as well as a woman) must have a heart in good working order. A healthy heart is a hungry heart. People with hungry hearts soon recognize Jesus as the sought-for Savior, the living, loving Lord who speaks our name and lets us know that it is He.

Before His crucifixion Jesus was talking to His disciples about His impending death. He was telling them that He must leave them, but that He would return in a new role to be with them always. The world would not recognize His nearness, but they would. "How is it," they inquired, "that You will show Yourself to us and not to the world?"

"If a person *loves* me," He answered, "he will guard my words," and He went on to show that such loving obedience would be the secret of their sensitiveness to His presence.

In weighing the evidence for the proposition that Jesus is alive and in the place of power at God's right hand, do not overlook the testimony of many lovers of Jesus who can tell you that their elemental heart hunger has been and continues to be satisfied perfectly by Him. There is, in other words, such a thing as a personal experience; yes, let us dare call it an *emotional* experience of Christ. Standing as it does between John's inquiring intellect and Thomas' stubborn will, Mary's emotion is guarded from becoming mere bathos. So may ours be. Purists in worship may turn up their noses at a song like "In the Garden." The verse is no great shakes, and the music is not Bach by any means, but it utters something which is important and legitimately Christian.

> "I come to the garden alone
>   While the dew is still on the roses
>   And the voice I hear, falling on my ear
>   The Son of God discloses."

He manifests His presence by the solid comfort He brings to the hungry heart.

3. *THOMAS in Turn Reminds Us of the Necessity of the Conquered Will*

"The Twin" was his original nickname, but "The Doubter" is the label which superseded it. Ordinarily when we speak of doubt, we have in mind intellectual difficulties posed by the vastness of our universe, or by the rampant evil which belies God's just government, or by the latest psychological explanation of the soul's "non-existence," or by modern man's bafflement with the language of the Bible. Thomas' doubts, however, would seem to have been much deeper than mere intellectual uneasiness. If you will check the several passages in which he appears on the Bible page, I think you will sense that his deepest discomfort is rooted in his disposition, rather than in his mind. They showed themselves in a certain stubborn pessimism which was his defense mechanism against what he had decided was a grim kind of world and a harsh sort of Heavenly Father.

There was in Thomas something of the spirit of the man in Jesus' parable who had organized his affairs on the assumption that his master was a hard man, demanding more than his due.

John's order in listing these three Resurrection Day encounters with Christ is climactic. Before man listens to his heart, he should be sure that his head is functioning — whether the subject is religion or romance! But it is true besides, that neither head nor heart can fully speak for us or finally convince us.

It is a strange and awe-full fact that one may be convinced intellectually that the Bible tells truth, and stirred emotionally to the point of hunger for God's peace, and yet that one may still be holding out against the claims of Jesus to be his Lord and God. The reason for his reservation may be mainly moral. Flaws in his character may call for critical attention which he is unwilling to risk. I know emotionally ill persons who want to be well but who fear the painful prospect of having to be utterly honest about themselves. Thomas may have cherished a particular vice. More likely he was an upright man, the defect of whose rectitude was the rigidity which accompanies virtue now and then. He may have been so constructed that decisions must always go his way "or else." In myself I think of it as the "Atlas Complex": a compulsive carrying of the weight of the whole world on one's shoulders, and a consequent despair of ever really succeeding at anything.

One thing is clear, however, about Thomas. Whatever the cause of his doubting, the cure lay in the surrender of his will to the One who had come to conquer it.

At times I have been troubled a little by the fact that after His resurrection, Jesus revealed Himself alive only to *disciples*. This could make the whole matter smell slightly fishy, don't you think? And inevitably the theory has been put forth that the disciples "saw" their friend Jesus in much the same manner that thirsty travelers see mirages in Sahara or non-existent oases. Longing mixed with hope can produce illusion. "The disciples saw what they wanted and half-expected to see." So runs the cynical verdict.

Like every other stock objection to the resurrection of Jesus, this one falls apart by its own structural weakness. The disciples ruefully remind us that they did *not* half-hope it would happen. They were frightened and dis-illusioned and hopeless and hard to convince. All of them shared something of Thomas' stubborn refusal to credit the reports until Jesus himself, patiently and personally, reinforced what had been told them.

What the limited scope of His resurrection appearances does illustrate is not the gullibility of believers but rather the moral quality of belief. Belief in the resurrection of Jesus, like belief in the existence of God himself, is practically impossible and essentially unstable unless at the decision-point of his inner existence a man is prepared to say "Yes!" to the Lord when He makes Himself known. This is not circular argument. It is the way persons discover other persons, and it is the way a man can find God.

Thomas' earlier absence when Jesus met with the rest may well have been a case of moral struggle and final moral decision. Was it his wilfulness which had kept him away the first time Jesus found them behind barred doors? And was it his sense of duty which drew him to the same place for the second, conclusive appointment? We may guess so. But there is no question whatever, as there was none in Thomas' mind by that time, what was expected of him before he could be fully reinstated.

The poet has phrased it well:

> "Our wills are ours, we know not how
> Our wills are ours to make them Thine!"

And was not Jesus enforcing much the same lesson for Thomas? He is to stop wanting things his way and to start willing everything Christ's way. Else he will continue to be a divided, defeated, doubtful person. So with his stubbornness shattered, down he goes at Jesus' feet to confess his willingness.

The pure in heart are the ones who see God. And purity of heart, as a seer has said, is to will one thing, namely, the will of God.

If God is unreal to you, the resurrection hope will be unreal too, and for the same reason. The Bible in that case will be a closed book, and prayer a matter of bouncing your faint hopes off the ceiling. The church will be irrelevant, and religious exercise a waste of time.

God cannot, or will not, be real to you until you are ready. Perhaps in desperation you will cry out to a still nameless Deity. Perhaps in sheer boredom and disgust with life you will attempt a prayer. "What is Your name?" "What *is* your game?" "What is this life all about?" "Who am I?" "What do you want me to do?" Ah, that last cry, if you mean it, is enough. If it is an honest inquiry, it will get an answer. And if you are within earshot of the Christian gospel, that answer will be in terms of Jesus Christ.

It may not at first be a Risen Christ whom you will meet and recognize as your Answer. It may well be the Man on the New Testament pages whose words ring true and whose deeds give you new hope. Sooner or later He will seem to be talking about you and to you and saying, "Well, how about it; what will you do with Me?"

Then if you decide to give Him a try, using whatever logic your mind can command, and with the hungry longing of your heart whispering, "Yes! Yes! — He is the One we need!" you are on your way to knowing the full story. You will begin to know Him as the Son of God and Savior, the Victor over death, and Coming King.

You and I live at the wrong time to make the journey with Peter and John to the sepulchre, or to greet Jesus in Joseph's garden with Mary Magdalene, or to be congregated with the eleven and confronted by His Majesty in their secret hiding place.

We are, however, promised something which He told His disciples would be far better and more permanent. We are promised the constant presence of our Christlike

God. He comes to us through the Holy Spirit to be resident among His people and to be involved in their lives.

The way to have this experience now is in essence just what it was then. You must look for Him with the best logic of your mind, the acknowledged hunger of your heart, and the glad surrender of your will.

Chapter III
Either/or

"But the angel said to the women, 'Do not be afraid; for I know that you seek Jesus who was crucified. He is not here; for he has risen, as he said. Come, see the place where he lay.'" — Matthew 28:5, 6

These first-century Christians who gave us our New Testament were sure as sure could be about the resurrection. They were sure because they had seen Jesus before and after. They had followed (afar off) and watched him die. They had cringed with the conclusive spear thrust. Some had helped take his cold body down and away to Joseph of Arimathea's tomb. They had watched the soldiers seal the tomb and had said, "Goodbye forever!"

Then came the glorious shock of the morning after the Sabbath, and the inexpressibly precious forty days of fellowship with their risen Lord — different, yet unmistakably He.

This sermon is reprinted by permission of *Theology and Life* magazine of which Dr. Vassady is editor.

Subsequent Christians have been assured too, but on a different basis. Jesus had anticipated this in His conversation with the doubter, Thomas. "Because you have seen you believe. Blessed are they who have not seen and yet have believed." The implication is that there are other ways of arriving at assurance than by employment of the five senses.

One special way is by what we call the sixth sense or intuition. I suspect that any one of us can tell of decisions made on the basis of an unshakable hunch: "That's the girl for me!" "This is the job I should accept!" "Here is someone I can trust!" And later events have confirmed that however peculiarly we arrived at the particular certainty, we were right.

Some will be satisfied with this method of arriving at spiritual truth even though proverbially it is a woman's way to depend on intuition. Women frequently guess right! And even for the male mentality, steering by the sixth sense in matters of the soul can be rewarding. If the religious instinct is uncomplicated by insincerity, it can lead a person to Jesus Christ as unerringly as the homing instinct of a honey bee. When His death for sinners and His glorious resurrection is preached (i.e., announced), such a person will find himself responding as did Helen Keller, the little blind and deaf girl, who, when first told about God, said: "I always knew there must be Someone like that. I just didn't know His name."

But others for whom neither the five senses nor the sixth sense will do, must come to their convictions about matters spiritual by what we call "common-sense," which is a sort of mixture of information, and intuition, and logic — with logic having, if not the last word, at least a large part in the decision.

I hope there will be something in what I have to say

for those who are accustomed to arrive at faith via the sixth sense, but I must admit that the line of thought I have in view is more for the person who prefers to travel the logical road. The scheme of our sermon is simple enough. The Christian proclamation that "Christ is Risen" faces us with several sets of alternatives — upon which it is possible to pass a logical judgment. There probably are other *either/ors*, but we shall content ourselves with three.

1. Either Resurrection or Deception
2. Either Resurrection or Disintegration
3. Either Resurrection or Demoralization

1. *Either Resurrection or Deception*

Many of the arguments pro and con about the resurrection of Jesus center in the question whether the New Testament account of what happened is to be trusted. For those who are of a mind to argue, there are carefully developed studies which deal with this issue and discuss in detail the question whether the New Testament writers knew what they were talking about, and whether they told the truth when they reported the empty tomb and the various appearances mentioned in the Gospels, I Corinthians, and the Book of Acts.

In the light of even the minimum scholarly consensus concerning the historical value of the New Testament, it seems clear that one must ultimately make a choice between believing that Jesus rose from the dead, or retreating to a conclusion that deception (whether conscious or unconscious; pious or vicious) was practiced by the people who gave us the gospel. The resurrection announcement raises first of all this issue of the dependability of Scripture.

Now there are those who hold that any such question is immaterial. The Bible for them is a hodgepodge of fact and fable; of inspired truth and of ill-contrived falsehoods. Consequently, the reader of the New Testament is poorly advised to take any part of it much more seriously than he would a historical novel which develops a fictitious plot against a background of commonly accepted history, or than a collection of tales which incorporate a lot of folk wisdom in a rather primitive form. On such analogies as these, one can take the reports of the resurrection of Jesus, along with His "miracles" and much of His teaching, as morally helpful literature with present day value, yet not be bothered unduly by questions of fact.

In this fairy-tale context, the story of the resurrection of Jesus might be taken as a cheerful echo of the springtime pattern in nature with her bursting buds and opening flowers, flowing sap and comforting sunshine. Or, more personally, the resurrection idea may suggest the incurable optimism which mankind likes to feel about itself. Is the race threatened by the bomb? Recall that humanity has often been down but never out! Nature delivers a blow that sets Homo Sapiens reeling, but he has developed a brain, and he can invent new weapons, tools, shelters, medicines, etc., and come bouncing back again.

Speaking of bouncing back, however, the Bible can be bouncy too! After somebody has carefully explained it away, it still refuses to be dismissed in its claims to be taken seriously as history. Do you remember hearing the story of the impertinent casualty on the battlefield who balked at being diagnosed as dead? It seems that an army doctor, accompanied by a sergeant of the Medical Corps, was checking over the victims of a recent engagement. Having recommended several more or less wounded men to the attention of the ambulancers, he came to one poor fellow lying motionless where he had dropped. "This one is dead," said the physician. The man opened his eyes and said weakly, "I'm not!" To which in accustomed sergeant style the non-com shouted, "Don't argue! If the doctor says you're dead, you're dead!"

The New Testament, however, simply will not lie down and die for us without argument. It declares itself to be quite different from historical novels and collected fairy tales. It demands to be taken seriously as history. Says one of its authors: "We have not followed cunningly devised fables, when we made known unto you the power and coming of our Lord Jesus Christ, but were eyewitnesses of His majesty." Said another: "That which we have seen and heard declare we unto you."

The history of the critical study of the New Testament is an encouraging one. Subjected to the most careful sifting, often by men who were disposed to disprove it, the Bible again and again has risen to challenge those who were trying to explain it away. Sir William Ramsey's conversion to Christianity as a consequence of his analysis of the New Testament in the light of archaeological discoveries, is well known. A more recent instance of the same is to be found in the book by the British lawyer, Frank Morison. He entitles it, "Who Moved the Stone," and in it confesses that he set out to dispel the Easter "myth" but ended up having written an apologetic for the literal bodily resurrection of our Lord based on an attorney's examination of the evidence.

We are not claiming that the argument for the Gospel's historicity are such as to kidnap unbelievers into the Kingdom. But what we arrive at eventually as an issue to be faced is the question whether it is possible to build a system of ethics, in which truth is a central virtue, on a foundation of deception. Saying that the disciples may have been self-deceived does not appeal to my common sense at this point any more than accusing them of being conscious liars. I think we must, in all fairness, insist that either the resurrection of Jesus is a fact of history or else admit that Christianity rests upon and grows out of an elaborate fraud. Logic has something to say to me about where I wish to stand on this issue.

2. *Either Resurrection or Disintegration*

The first *either/or* had to do with our thinking about the Holy Bible. This second one deals with our concept of a human being. It is, I think, the same question whether we are speaking of the resurrection of Jesus Christ nearly nineteen-and-a-half centuries ago, or whether we have in view the resurrection of the bodies of believers which, according to New Testament teaching, is to take place when Jesus Christ comes into His Kingdom at the end of this era of God's program. As Paul points out in I Corinthians 15, if the resurrection of all believers is not conceivable, logically, neither is Jesus' rising from the dead. We might add, "and vice-versa"!

We are now discussing the idea of the resurrection of the body as a physical likelihood and are asking in effect whether it is a necessary or even a desirable concept in terms of our modern understanding of man.

Some would answer promptly in the negative. From the beginnings of Christianity, there were those who scoffed at the very idea. When the Apostle Paul visited Athens and preached on the topics of Jesus and the resurrection, he got blank stares or not too carefully muffled jeers from local professors of philosophy. For them the thought of a resurrection body was crude and unwelcome. Their image of human "being" at its best involved the sloughing off of one's body and an existence in the realm of "pure spirithood." And the Greek prejudice has persisted to this day, setting spirit over against body as elemental enemies of one another. Man's best hope, according to this view, is to lose his body in the grave while his spirit wings its way to heaven, if there is one, or into the memory museum of mankind at least. Something of the sort is what is often meant when people talk about the immortality of the soul.

Church members, perhaps unconsciously nurtured in the Greek tradition, have confessed to their pastor that they gag and fall silent when our Apostle's Creed bids us declare that we believe in "the resurrection of the *body,* and the life everlasting" since these two phrases sound to them mutually contradictory. Since it is commonly thought that the soul is immortal and the body mortal, why attempt to cramp the soaring spirit with another body when you are preparing it for paradise?

Tell me, have you never wished yourself rid of that burdensome body of yours, if you could do it without dying, so that you might sail where the magic carpet of imagination often takes you, over the treetops and across the ocean; out to the nearest planet or the farthest star? Have you never cursed your aches and pains, your blundering tongue, your middle-age complex of bridge-work, bifocals, and misplaced bulges? Who would not want to be independent of the toll time takes? Ancient legend is replete with fairy godmothers who reward the deserving with a touch which makes them invisible, invincible, able to go anywhere and do anything their little hearts desire. If death were to bring that liberation, it would be sweet indeed. So the Greeks reasoned from man's dreams to his probable destiny as a free, immortal soul.

The Greek mind, however, had its blind spot. It lacked the help which modern neurology could have given. It forgot that spirit cannot function without embodiment. Even the philosopher's lofty thoughts were not pure spirit as he imagined, for before one's thoughts can get off the ground they need a brain to use. And without modern medical instruments they might have guessed this by observing what happens to a person's thinking when he gets hit on the skull. Such evidence implies that you cannot separate body from spirit in a man and still have personality. If his body dies, and no new one is provided, the spirit will be deaf and dumb and blind and hopelessly imprisoned.

We use the word "integration" to describe among other things the cooperation of the various parts of a human being — physical, mental, spiritual, and social — in true harmony. Distintegration, then, means the breaking apart of a person so that he can no longer function as a whole. Therefore the Apostle Paul says, what modern physiology helps us to appreciate, that there is a "natural" body which dies and disintegrates, but there is to be a "spiritual" *body* which can reclothe the soul and integrate it as could never be possible under the old arrangement.

The Greeks were after the right goal, namely the capacity of a man to go where his imagination can go, and to do what his imagination would love to do. But Biblical realism calls for two indispensable conditions before this longing of ours can be allowed: First, the conquest of sin which perverts the imagination and makes it want to do degrading things; and Second, the destruction of death which leaves the spirit marooned without a vehicle for self-expression. The only logical way I can see for God to deal with this twin problem is by resurrection. Resurrection or Disintegration is the second grave issue.

3. *Either Resurrection or Demoralization*

The first *either/or* was about the Bible. The second had to do with our being. This one concerns our behavior. And here once more we may have both Jesus' resurrection and our own in mind. For instance, one of the strong arguments for belief in His resurrection is the behavioral change which took place in the disciples after they became convinced that he was literally alive again. When they turned away from the cross, they were submerged in hopelessness. The logic of their position was most baldly represented in Judas, who, seeing tragedy approaching, decided to make a little money out of it.

The demoralization Jesus' death brought is typified, too, in Peter. He was no traitor or profiteer, but an idealist who crumpled when the pressure was on. Such were the others who took to their heels that black Friday, as well as the two on the road to Emmaus who were ready to give up. They all illustrate the *either/or* about which we are here speaking. If death puts a tragic stop to men like Jesus, then their mood is appropriate. And it will become ours, too, in these fright-fraught times. "Demoralization" may speak of the collapse of morals or of morale, or both. "If in this life only we have hope in Christ," writes Paul, "we are of all men most miserable (demoralized)."

There are those who would challenge the Pauline principle that minus resurrection, human life is wretched, and the Christian way ridiculously so. (Perhaps it is good now and then for Christians to have their easy assumptions challenged, or else we make faith's answer sound too mechanical!) Recently I had a long conversation with an intelligent, articulate member of our city's Jewish community. I was surprised and rather startled at the casual way in which this person said to me, "You know, we liberal Jews do not believe in an after life." And then, a few sentences later, "And we are a happy people. We are not oppressed with fears of a God who will punish us with hell, any more than we are made anxious by a God who may or may not reward us with heaven." I did not argue then and am not arguing now, but I must say that in other parts of the conversation there were comments which unconsciously betrayed a great deal of anxiety and fear and disillusionment with life. This, for instance: "We Jews, when we think of the awful injustices that have been perpetrated on us, can only ask 'Why?'" And again: "Sometimes when I think of the kind of world we live in, I don't think I can hang onto hope much longer!"

To pick a person's logic to pieces when he is not around is very simple. And it is a temptation for preachers to oversimplify the relation between belief in the life to come and a person's moral stamina. Some of the most upright and genuinely kind people profess not to believe in God or heaven — at least not with their conscious minds. They may continue to act like Christians long after they have ceased to think as Christians. Perhaps family tradition rather than a living faith; inertia not *agape*, is what keeps them honorable.

Paul, however, persists in looking at the matter logically. "If in this life only we have hope in Christ we are *Les Miserables!*" ". . . if the dead rise not, let us eat and drink; for tomorrow we die." Emphasis is on the *we*. Animals are not wretched just because among philosophers there is some doubt whether a dog heaven or a cow heaven exists. If they are regularly tended and fed, they are content. Even man, when he has conditioned himself to a comfortable middle-way of a-morality ("I'll leave you alone if you leave me alone; I'll scratch your back if you'll scratch mine . . .") may not need an after life to keep him superficially cheerful and reasonably consistent.

Easy-going, self-centered people can "get along" apparently without an after life of resurrection. In fact, the thought of anything beyond is likely to scare them since they may sense that something more than their easy-going, self-centeredness would be required of them in a world which is the prep-school for the next.

But if you were a disciple, and if you had reorganized your life around the one whose name is Jesus; if you had taken His life as your standard of true personhood, and His law of love as the rule of your behavior — then if you were to find out that there is nothing beyond the grave for you; and especially if there was nothing beyond the cross for Jesus except a sepulchre, you would be a fool to keep on the narrow path. You might be a noble fool, but you would still be a fool. You would have invested your treasure in a non-existent gold mine. Anyone would be Quixotic, or neurotic (a modern way of saying the same thing), to persist in such a crazy quest!

Please do not counter at this point with any such theological nonsense as this for instance — that "while Jesus' body lay still in the tomb, His noble spirit lived on into the ages." Do not put us off with the euphemism that "a gallant human life endures forever in the memory of posterity." Such sentiments make nice poetry, perhaps, but they are loose in their logic. Either God is down to earth or He is not. Either the Christian life is morally realistic or it is a waste of time. Christian morality and Christian morale being what they are, the issue would seem to be: either Resurrection or Demoralization.

* * *

Well, the theme of New Testament preaching is resurrection, construed not poetically but literally. Jesus' cold, dead body was touched with creative power by the One who invented biochemistry and who originated life. It was transmuted into a perfect instrument for Jesus' immortal spirit. It passed through the grave clothes without

having to unwrap them, and through the unsealed tomb
door. (The stone was rolled away by heavenly messengers
so that the disciples could look in, and see, and believe —
not so Jesus could get out!)

He companied with the skeptical, bewildered disciples
for forty days, eating in their presence, opening to them
the Scriptures, and instructing them in the technique of
living their Christian lives in dependence upon the Holy
Spirit. Then He left them for an indeterminate while, in
order at the last to come again in power and great glory
and usher in the resurrection of all His people.

Christ is risen indeed!

This is the Christian announcement. This is the Biblical
alternative to the deception, the disintegration, the
demoralization with which otherwise, quite logically, we
should have to reckon.

Chapter IV

Our Recognition of His Presence

"They said to each other, 'Did not our hearts burn within us while he talked to us on the road, while he opened to us the scriptures?' " — Luke 24:32

We have here not only the account of something which took place on the evening of the first Easter, but a parable of what can happen in the life of any Christian in any age or season.

By definition, a parable is "an earthly story with a heavenly meaning." It could include equally well an *historical incident* with a spiritual meaning. Our conviction of the trustworthiness of the New Testament leads us to believe that this encounter with the risen Christ actually occurred, literally and visibly. But I believe it is told us as a parable of the sort of Christian experience we may expect today, though we can see Him no longer with the eye of flesh.

An historical incident with a spiritual meaning? By "spiritual" we do not mean *imaginary*. Some would go along too easily with our thesis. "Oh yes, I believe that Christ is with us in a spiritual sense." But when you press to discover what is meant by the word "spiritual," it appears that He is to be thought of as present through the medium of our imagination. If that were all, then our title would be misleading, and the New Testament itself would be gutted of all substantial importance. If by Christ's spiritual presence you mean only a feeling we get when we think about Him, analogous to the inspiration one finds in reading about Pheidippides, or Plato, or Paul, then we are talking about two different matters.

But Jesus taught His disciples, repeating it over and over again, that while He would leave them so far as visibility was concerned, He could and would continue to be with them in a new dimension, provided they were properly prepared. He would be not less really present, but, inconceivable as it might sound, more so. Instead of being limited to visibility of a quarter mile or so, and to audibility for perhaps three thousand pairs of ears at once, He would be able to be with them always, everywhere, even to the end of the age. Just do not expect to eat your cake and have it too. We cannot have Him with us everywhere, anytime, and all at once, yet still demand that He be visible!

If a person does not believe in God, or in the reality of the human soul, then such a concept as this is sheer nonsense. But if we do believe in the dimension we call "spirit" with respect to God and to ourselves, however little we understand the processes, we may credit the promises. And what we are talking about in analyzing this parable of spiritual truth is, in consequence, reasonable to discuss.

Add to this theoretical point the practical consideration that we have testimony from a vast number of Christians concerning Christ as the most real and compelling force in their lives. Maybe in the light of what they say, we can be open minded enough to give serious heed to the principles our parable proposes in order to recognize His presence.

1. *Notice That These Two on the Road to Emmaus Were TOGETHER*

"And it came to pass that while they communed together and reasoned, Jesus himself drew near and went with them."

There is a certain magic in company, and particularly in the company of kindred minds. There is something about being together in a cause which makes two people more than twice as strong as one, and three more than three times as strong, and so on. In union there is strength, and in a crowd men find courage. How good it is for one's morale to enter a crowded church for worship or to have standing room only at a midweek service. I have heard of an occasional congregation where it happens! Even a comfortably full sanctuary on Sunday sends us home in a bit of a glow.

But what we have been picturing may be largely subjective and psychological. It may have to do with religious feeling more than with spiritual fact. A crowd in itself is no guarantee of the presence of the Lord. He does indicate, however, in various of His sayings that He wills to be present in a special way where there is a fellowship of concerned Christian persons. Just two are enough to fulfil the numerical condition: "Where two or three are gathered in my name, there am I in the midst." "If two of you are agreed," as to prayer it "shall be granted."

He does not ignore the solitary. The Gospels show Him singling out individuals for attention. Several of the resurrection appearances were to audiences of one — to

Mary Magdalene, to Peter, to James, and not least to Saul who was untimely born, but marked no less for apostleship.

However, most of His appearances were to groups. I sense some import here. The Good Shepherd seeks the lone, lost lamb, but it is to bring it back to the comfort of the flock. We are warned by the Word not to forsake the assembling of ourselves together as is the manner of some religious loners, but instead to encourage one another and to provoke (sharpen up) one another unto love and good works. When we pray we are to seek God's face in company with others. "When ye pray say *our* Father!"

In mere association there is no necessary spiritual value, but if by our communion we are stirred up into a concern, a deeper, keener, more informed concern, then it has great worth. Such was the mood of the two men en route to Emmaus. They were spiritual sparring partners; they were playing a mournful game of catch. "What sort of communications," the mysterious Stranger who had joined them was asking, "do you *antiballete* (the Greek word means literally 'to toss back and forth')?" That was His question. And they told Him just what. It was not the weather nor the economic trend. They had been talking together concerning Jesus of Nazareth.

A pastor frequently comes across people who profess to feel not the least bit dependent upon fellowship with other Christians. They claim to find more inspiration alone on a mountaintop, or involved with a trout stream, or at their own Bible reading and bedside prayer. They are annoyed by what seems to them the exaggerated emphasis among conventional Christians upon church-going and organizational church activities. They can get just as close to God alone! So? Admitted already that there is no automatic spirituality in a random collection of folk, even if

Christians. But if it happens to be an aggregation of the spiritually concerned, there is bound to be a mutual stimulation, a cross-fertilizing process, making available insights which one does not get when attempting to go it alone.

Participation in prayer meetings, for instance, when intercession goes round the informal circle invariably is a revelation to me. I do not easily participate. Prayer shyness is a family trait! But I cannot remember any such gathering, and there have been many, where someone's prayer, however fumbling, did not introduce a novel, helpful idea into my own prayer-experience.

So one must ask the Christian isolationist not only the obvious question: "Are you doing anything to share your experience of God with others?" but also this more profound one: "Is it really He who finds you out there all by yourself? Or is it just the moody Mother Nature of paganism who caresses today and stabs you tomorrow? Do you very often get an experience of the reality of Jesus Christ all by yourself without the stimulus and discipline of the redeemed family of God which is the church? I have reason to doubt whether you do!"

The characteristic impulse of the crucifixion instant was to scatter. The mood of Easter morning and thereafter, a mood which settled into the habit pattern of the early church, was expressed by assemblage. And it was while they were together, praying and praising, on the Day of Pentecost that the Holy Spirit came in power according to promise and with the precision which made them sure that Jesus Christ was in their midst again.

2. *Observe Again That They Were Engaged IN BIBLE STUDY*

"And beginning at Moses and all the prophets, he expounded unto them in all the scriptures the things concerning himself . . .

'Did not our hearts burn within us as he walked with us and opened to us the scriptures?' "

If a time machine could turn back clock and calendar and permit you to share one scene from the New Testament with Jesus in the days of His flesh, which would you choose? I think perhaps I would pick the Emmaus road, though I cannot fully explain why. History was my college major, and maybe it is the thought of listening to the meaning of world history being unfolded by its Author, "of whom and through whom and unto whom are all things, who is the Alpha and the Omega; the Beginning and the End." The verb "expounded" is in the Greek imperfect tense and indicates that He went on interpreting, moving from passage to passage. Piece after piece fitted into place like a complicated puzzle in the hands of its inventor, or like an infinitely delicate and involved mechanism. How I wish I had been with them then!

But actually we are not nearly as remote from this experience as we might think. At least we need not be. For if there is anything evident in the New Testament, it is that the disciples of the risen Lord did not envision the church as a secret society or the gospel as a deep, dark mystery for a few initiates only. At His predictive command they waited for a matter of seven weeks and then began to go everywhere proclaiming the unveiled meaning of Scripture to any who would listen. To be sure, they were human and fallible, but they had the Holy Spirit to wing their words and to keep them loyal to the original Word. Then, as time passed and the needs of the churches became apparent, they wrote down what Jesus had said to them so as not to lose one precious syllable. We may be quite sure that the gist of the conversation along the Emmaus road found its way directly and exactly into the New Testament. Of course, it would have been more exciting to get it from the lips of Jesus. But the Holy Spirit still makes the whole thing come to light and come alive for the man who earnestly searches the Scriptures.

So here is the second stage in one's recognition of His presence. Jesus opened the meaning of the Old Testament to these men not just for their information, that they might become famous Biblical scholars; not merely for their encouragement, either, though that was a glad by-product of the main intent. But chiefly to get them ready to recognize Him. They were soon to see that it was He, as their physical eyes were loosed from temporary hindrance. He was preparing them also to be sure of His invisible presence all the rest of their lives. "O dull of perception and slow of heart," He was saying to them, "was it not fitting for the Christ to suffer these things, and equally suitable for Him to enter into that new and more luminous relationship with His people — which is His glory?" Such was the gist of His words to them. And these words are for us, too.

Do you want to know as a Christian today why things happen the way they do in the world, and why matters go as they do in your own life? Do you want to know what or who it is in you that makes you hungry for righteousness, and unhappy in the grip of sin; deeply glad when you are right with God and relieved when you honestly face yourself and repent? Do you want to understand why your strength is as the strength of ten when your heart is pure, and why nothing goes right when it is not? Do you want to grasp the meaning of life in this era of meaninglessness and mass despair? Then go to the Bible.

But do not go just for information so that you can preen. Go expecting to get wisdom, and remember that the fear of the Lord (which is an ancient way of saying "sensitiveness to His holy presence") is the beginning of wisdom. Job's deep and desperate and most contemporary questions were answered only as God Himself drew near and revealed Himself. And Jesus' deliverance of two disillusioned travelers headed for Emmaus was not the result of bare Bible study. It was opening the Scriptures with the end in view of introducing Himself.

Then let us not be impatient or unexpectant in our Bible study. And let us not imagine that when we have heard the preacher out, or been instructed by our Sunday School teacher, "thus endeth the lesson." The knowledge of Scripture is not an end in itself, ever. It is a means to the end we have been describing: that is, the recognition of the Lord's presence.

For most of us it is the only practicable means. Who would not like to take the mystic's short-cut? Who would not relish traveling by sheer vaulting emotion into the very Presence of God? India is the home of the wistful fakir who resolves to take heaven by storm either through rapt contemplation or self-torture. Sundhar Singh, the Christian Sadhu, tells how he traveled up and down India asking these countrymen of his, "Have you found what you seek?" Many were annoyed to be so challenged; a few were sadly honest. None could do better than to express a vague hope that perhaps, in some reincarnation, their patience might pay off. Mysticism minus the Bible is a blind alley. It is Jesus Christ for whom the human heart hungers, and, said the great Blaise Pascal, who was something of a mystical genius himself but knew his limitations, "He is to be found in the ways taught in the Gospel."

What? Is God dependent upon paper and printers' ink, on dotted i's and crossed t's to reveal Himself? Is He bound to the Bible? Why should I have to plod through Leviticus, or wrestle with the complicated sentence structure of Paul? Not because God is limited, so much as because we are. Why can we not shortcut into scientific discovery, or musical mastery, by the mystic's way? Why fuss with two-plus-two and pi-R-squared; with do-re-mi and dull finger drills? The obvious answer is that until we are willing to plod, we cannot soar. Until we have wrestled with the letter of Scripture, we cannot walk with the Lord in the Spirit. An understanding, however elementary, of God's written Word is a second stage in discovering the reality of Christ's presence with us. The symptom of His nearness is not a spooky tingle of the spinal nerve. It is the burning of our hearts as the Bible opens to us.

3. *See, thirdly, That the Two on the Emmaus Road Were at PRAYER*

"But they constrained him, saying, 'Abide with us; for it is toward evening, and the day is far spent.' And he went in to tarry with them."

Can you find anywhere a more perfect prayer than this? The hymn writer saw it as such and took the verse and simply expanded it into one of the loveliest and most expressive prayer hymns of the church.

Some have the notion that to be an effective pray-er you must have a lot of "faith," and that in order to have a lot of "faith" you must feel very sure of God. And so one becomes involved in a kind of vicious circle of prayer-lessness. Not seeing clearly we do not pray. Not praying we see less clearly. Gradually we find that in place of childhood's sureness, we have an adult loneliness and alienation from our Maker.

"I remember, I remember the fir-trees dark and high;
I used to think their slender tops were close against the sky.
It was a childish ignorance, but now 'tis little joy
To know I'm farther off from heaven than when I was a boy."

According to the New Testament, however, faith is its
own evidence of things not as yet seen. In other words
it is a kind of instinct, like the homing inerrancy of the
migratory bird. It is an instinct complicated somewhat
by the fact that being human, we can inspect, and doubt,
and deny our inner wisdom instead of responding to it.
Still, an instinct has its own strange authority, and there
is no dishonesty in starting to pray before we are sure to
whom we are praying. The question is one of sincerity
at this point. Are we actually looking for light, tracking
truth? Our custom of closing eyes to pray may be misleading to scoffers. We close our eyes not to avoid the
light of truth but that we may tune in more precisely the
light which comes on another wave-length than the
optical. The gentleman at the symphony who seems to be
asleep and dreaming conceivably of the cash-register or
of the customer may rather be shutting his eyes to open
all the wider his capacity for concentrating on the tide
of beauty which pours over him out from the orchestra.

True prayer is a turning in the direction of a light we
have seen or begun to sense.

These men still did not know who this was who walked
and talked with them. Part of His resurrection body's new
power seems to have been to screen itself subtly from
their premature recognition. They did not yet know Him,
but they knew that He had something they needed, and
they begged for more of it. The value of their prayer was
not in its certitude but in its sincerity. They "constrained
Him" — whether by force of grasp or by intensity of tone
we are not told. Prayer is just this: a genuine invitation
for the Lord to enter into our lives and to abide with us,
especially as the shadows lengthen all down the little
landscape of our life.

There are ways, incidentally, of inviting company which

can display a lack of genuine cordiality. Our friends may not always be sensitive enough to realize that while they are welcome in a way, it will be good news to mine host if they do not linger! (Missus was planning to give herself a home permanent. The Mister had a hobby going in the cellar workshop.) But there are no such mental reservations at Emmaus. These travelers are tired, and they are hungry, but they are hungrier yet to hear more of what He has to say. It is a wonder that they think to set bread before Him. Maybe they did not. Perhaps, as at the Galilean shore a few days later with the Eleven, He had to ask these two whether they were not famished and, if so, whether there was anything edible about?

Their manners may well have been questionable, but their hospitality was sincere. They expressed it as a prayer, and their prayer was heeded. He came in, and He broke bread with that characteristic mannerism, after He, too, had prayed, giving thanks. "And their eyes were opened, and they knew Him . . . ."

The prayer for light, for understanding, for one's share of Heaven's wisdom is always answered. The answer may not necessarily be on the terms we propose, and it may not be as immediately apparent as our impatient self-love would like. Nor will it always soothe and comfort us with a tranquil hearthside happiness and sweet dreams to follow. The answer to the Easter evening prayer of these two disciples sent them running, weary as they were, all the way back to Jerusalem to tell their story to a rather incredulous lot of others.

I cannot predict what strenuous new responsibilities the answer to your request for light may lay upon you. I just know that when Christians are together, really involved in Bible study and prayer, Jesus Himself draws near and goes with them and responds to their earnest invitation by revealing His presence and authenticating His parting promise in a most personal way:

"Lo, I am with you alway, even to the end of the age!"

Chapter V

Beyond Bewilderment

"And he said to them, 'Do not be amazed; you seek Jesus of Nazareth, who was crucified. He has risen, he is not here; see the place where they laid him. But go, tell his disciples and Peter that he is going before you to Galilee; there you will see him, as he told you.'"

Mark 16:6, 7

The word Mark uses to describe the reaction of the disciples to the events of Easter is an unusual one. The King James Version fails to reflect it clearly, saying simply that they were "affrighted" or afraid. The Revised Standard Version comes closer: "They were *amazed*," it reports. But even that does not do justice to the original Greek. Nowadays we find all sorts of items "amazing," like detergents and cake-mixes and circus side-shows and the gas consumption of compact cars.

Mark's word is picturesque and powerful. It hints that the disciples were only a step or two away from collapse. They were terror-stricken, disoriented, and disorganized.

They were what slanguage would call "in a complete tiz-
zy." A more dignified synonym would be "bewildered."

Who would not be bewildered! Their tidy little universe
had just been blown to bits, and a brand new one had
been plunked down in its place over the weekend. Their
smoothly spinning globe had suddenly gone into reverse,
and they felt it slipping out from under their feet while
they scratched and scrambled like lumberjacks on a
spinning log trying to keep their equilibrium. And when
God's messenger met them at the tomb of Joseph of
Arimathea, where Jesus' body should have been and was
not, and this strange young man in a white garment said:

> "Do not be bewildered . . .,"

it must have sounded as unreasonable a piece of advice
as for the steward of an ocean liner in a hurricane to say
to a seasick passenger, "Please stop rocking the boat!"

> "Do not be bewildered . . . ."

The more they thought about this advice afterward, the
more, however, they must have come to appreciate that
it had been the word they needed that early Easter morning. So they told us all about it:

> "Do not be bewildered," said the man in white, "Ye seek Jesus
> of Nazareth, who was crucified; He is risen; He is not here:
> behold the place were they laid Him. But go your way, tell his
> disciples and Peter that he goeth before you into Galilee; there
> shall ye see Him, as He said unto you."

This more detailed directive might be summarized in
four short words which, if we will heed them, can take us
beyond bewilderment this Easter Sunday to the kind of
peaceful, powerful, permanent assurance about the living
Christ which every one of His disciples should have.

The words: *Think!* . . . *Check!* . . . *Talk!* . . . *Seek!*

1. *THINK!*

"Ye seek *Jesus of Nazareth,* who was crucified: He is risen."

Here, into the mental blankness and emotional chaos of these women, comes a familiar and comforting sound. It is the name of Jesus and the mention of His home town. One may well imagine that the three words, "Jesus of Nazareth," were like the sound of a familiar melody in the ears of a wanderer far from home, bringing with it a flood of wholesome memories.

I can recollect from college days certain classes in which it seemed that the professor was taking a savage delight in hacking my faith to pieces in his lectures. He appeared to be so very brilliant and unanswerable in his logic. Who would dare to disagree! Now, as I look back into my college yearbook, I can realize that he was not then much older than our eldest child, a few years out of school. The arguments he used were often one-sided, conditioned, I suppose, by his own emotional reactions against authority. But to John Freshman it was as if the sun had been shot down from the heavens. What had felt like solid ground underfoot had melted into quicksand. I was losing my faith. "Is there anything left for a fellow to believe?" one began to wonder.

And then, somehow, the name of Jesus of Nazareth found its way into my consciousness. It was like a hand stretched out to steady and to lift. I decided that whatever else might be taken away, Jesus of Nazareth was to be followed. He is worth living and dying for. Such a relief to find a foundation on which to start building again; to see a ray of light toward which to move!

After awhile, piece by piece, the New Testament faith returned, and fitted together, and formed an intelligible and satisfying whole. It became evident that the sarcastic young professor had been demolishing, not God, but some stuffed scarecrows to which he had pinned the god-label. Confusion and terror and bewilderment had been very real, but the name of Jesus proved to be the antidote.

> "How sweet the name of Jesus sounds
> In a believer's ear!
> It soothes his sorrow, heals his wounds
> And drives away his fear.
>
> Dear Name the rock on which I build,
> My shield and hiding place;
> My never failing treasury, filled
> With boundless stores of grace!"

One does not, however, need to wait for times of spiritual shock to appreciate the importance of thinking about Jesus. It is meant to be our daily exercise in orientation. There are enough threatening things awaiting us as we roll out of bed and begin to get organized any day in the year. Happy is the man who has learned not to step out the front door until he has established his true position, not alone in terms of clock, or calendar, or map, but in the light of a Christ-centered creed:

> "I believe in God, the Father Almighty — and in Jesus Christ His only Son our Lord!"

and of a Christ-taught prayer:

> "Our Father which art in heaven, Hallowed be Thy name;
> Thy kingdom come, Thy will be done
> On earth as it is in heaven!"

What has all this to do with Easter? Much in every way! Belief in the resurrection of Jesus and the hope concerning our own heavenly destination which is so closely connected with it — these are not awkward afterthoughts for Christians. They are the logical consequence from our *knowledge in Jesus Christ* of the kind of God we worship.

If it could be at this time that I am speaking to some who find it hard to credit the New Testament proclamation of a risen Christ, might I suggest that you begin neither with the laws of biology or physics nor even with the phenomena of psychology which are unquestionably a part of the problem of accepting such a miracle. Begin instead with a good, long look at the Person whom the New Testament introduces. When you have kept company with Him awhile, I can predict that you will find yourself musing: "Well, if anyone ever deserved to break the death-barrier, it was He. For Him, vindication by resurrection would be most appropriate!" Now you are on your way to New Testament type faith; for the first corrective to bewilderment is to *think*, with Jesus of Nazareth as the object of your earnest attention.

2. CHECK!

"He is not here, behold the place where they laid him."

Mark does not tell us as much as the other Gospel writers about what was to be seen inside the empty tomb where Jesus' body had been. Mark is always in a hurry, and I am glad that others came along to supplement his brief account with more details. John lets us know about the grave-clothes, those heavy winding sheets soaked with ointments and spices, within which devoted friends of the dead would wind his corpse until it was encased, when dry, almost as by a plaster cast. John reports that when he and Peter came to the empty sepulchre and looked in, they found the grave clothes still wrapped and formed for Jesus' body, but *empty* as if the corpse had completely evaporated. And there are other evidential details which one may investigate by means of directed reading in any good theological library.

What is important for us now, in the brief time before

us, is to recognize that the Christian faith, unlike some others, is not insulated against the investigation of its credentials. I find an intimation of this in Mark's report of the command we have just quoted. The women are told to look into the tomb and be sure. One catches the same note at the beginning of the Gospel when the new teacher replies to inquirers, "Come, and see!" This open attitude is to be found throughout the New Testament; and it informs all of what we call Christian experience.

The authors of the New Testament insist that they are not recounting the sort of interior visions which can entertain a dreamer of strange dreams while his dormitory-mate hears only snoring or sighs! "That which we have seen and heard, which our hands have handled," is what the Apostles are testifying about. As Paul says to King Agrippa in his noteworthy defense:

> "The King knoweth of these things, before whom also I speak freely, for I am persuaded that none of these things are hidden from him, for this thing was not done in a corner" (Acts 26:26).

Well said! And may it be more frankly admitted among us. Either Christianity can stand the light, or it is a lie. And its central thesis is that Jesus came in the flesh, and lived and died and rose again bodily and actually — not mythologically or in someone's pious wish.

What is true about the Easter message is true about all the other doctrines which surround it. They are intended to be checked. We are not saying that all of the claims of Christianity are susceptible to the sort of proof which would make it impossible for anyone to disbelieve. We can recognize that God would not gain much if he made men good by force. And it is appropriate that good belief, as well as good behavior, should involve free choice between real alternatives. Whether we like it or not, the laws of relationships between persons are not as readily "proved" as mathematical propositions are. The man who waits for absolute evidence that he has found the perfect mate before he gets married should learn to cook! And no one is going to be able to convince you against your will that Jesus rose bodily from the dead, or that the New Testament is trustworthy, or even that God exists, for that matter. What we are insisting is that there is adequate testimony to the resurrection of the kind that will stand up under scrutiny. The person who troubles to check can be intellectually honest and spiritually sure when he comes in the Creed to where it says: "The third day He rose again from the dead."

3. *TALK!*

"But go your way, *tell* his disciples and Peter that he goeth before you into Galilee."

In order fully to appreciate the bearing of these words we need, again, to read not only Mark's brief account but those of the other evangelists and of Paul as well. When we do, we shall begin to get the cumulative impact of the appearances of Jesus after His rising. There is a whole series of encounters and conversations so that when the scattered followers of Jesus came together, they found that each of them had a separate piece of the puzzle and that the various pieces all fitted together into a picture with only one possible meaning:

"He is risen, indeed!"

One of the favorite theories proposed by those who would disprove the Biblical account is that "hysteria" among the disciples, shocked as they were by the brutal murder of their Messiah, produced the fantastic notion that He had not died after all. As thirsty travelers in the

desert think they see oases, or as men caught in the
squeeze of ruthless social pressures may develop neurotic
delusions, so these shocked idealists imagined for themselves a resurrection event.

There is a touch of plausibility here, as anyone who has
dealt with mental illness will recognize. The theory begins
to fall apart, however, with our discovery that the experience of fellowship with the risen Christ was claimed
not just by one or two tearful women at the tomb, but by
various others in widely differing places and circumstances, totalling, as Paul tells us, literally hundreds of
witnesses before the weeks between Passover and Pentecost were past. People do not hallucinate en masse! And
there are other commonsense reasons why it is really
harder to believe the hysteria theory than to accept the
New Testament at its face value.

Just now, however, our interest is more in the symbolic
lesson of the angel's advice, "Go and tell what you have
seen." As the women gather with the others to hear their
reports of meetings with the Lord, their bewilderment
begins to give way to hope.

We have a reminder here concerning the importance
of the church in the Christian's life. Christianity has its
centrifugal aspect. It throws out its sparks of light, its
missionaries ordained and spontaneous, into all the world
for the sharing of the news of Jesus. But it has also its cen-
tripetal tug. The two forces are, in fact, in constant alterna-
tion like the motion of a football team — first the huddle
and then the attack; first the gathering and then the
scattering. To those unfamiliar with football or with
religion such shifts may be mystifying. Among church
people, however, the regular rhythm of grouping and
deploying makes good sense.

Here too is a suggestion of the vital importance of

Christian *talk*. We gather at church for talk among ourselves, and then we go out into the week of work, school,
or recreation and talk with others, in word or deed, about
our faith. At times we may wonder concerning the value
of all the talk. Words seem so insubstantial in a world
of hard facts and dynamic forces, but let us not minimize
their power. Marriages fail not for lack of sex or of finan-
cial security but because couples fail to talk. Wars smolder
and burst into flame when men become disgusted with
diplomacy and stop talking. Faith in God falters, and
Christians stumble over minor obstacles because of failure
to keep communication with other believers and one's
withdrawal into the little private world of one's worries,
self-pity, and self-doubt.

It was good advice for the bewildered then, and it is
still. "Go, find the others. Tell your story and listen to
theirs. Witness and be witnessed to." This is not weakness.
It is wisdom, and it will bring reassurance.

4. *SEEK!*

"There shall ye see him, as he said unto you."

In the end what the disciples needed, whether or not
they knew it yet, was not just to *feel* better about things
but to find Jesus and to begin the new relationship with
Him, no longer "according to the flesh" but, quoting Paul
again, as "Christ in you, the hope of glory."

This new dimension of experience was not to be fully
theirs until after Jesus had ascended to the Father and
the Holy Spirit had come in a special way on the day of
Pentecost. Meanwhile it was of utmost importance that
they should be with their Master for a period of intensive
instruction so that He could draw together and summarize
all He had to teach them about Himself. He would instruct
them too about the transition from His dwelling with

them visibly and bodily to the life He would live in them through the Holy Spirit. So for forty days they all went back to school with Him. They learned more in those forty days than they had managed to absorb in the previous three years, because at last they were contrite, and teachable, and trusting.

The Christian faith is not so much a philosophy as a friendship. We are slow to acquiesce in this, perhaps because holding an opinion is less demanding upon us than cultivating a relationship, especially with a disturbing person like Jesus. Being a good Christian is not just subscribing to a correct creed, or even maintaining a proper conduct. It is entering into and enjoying a life-transforming companionship. So it is important for you and me to discover the reality of Jesus' resurrection not just in order to be orthodox, worthy as that is. The reason it is important is not even in order that our life may find its meaning and so that death can have no terrors. These are by-products of Christian experience. They are not of its essence.

The supreme reason for us to accept the New Testament announcement of a living Savior is to prepare us to seek and find Him as our personal Friend. Our creeds have value only if they introduce us to this possibility. Our behavior is authentically Christian only as it makes clear that we belong to Him.

Here, probably, is the place to raise a very personal question. What exactly are you looking for in church this Easter day?

I read somewhere a sermon on the text, "Seek and ye shall find!" Who preached it, I cannot recall, but I remember being impressed by it because the author was insisting that this word of Jesus means precisely what it says. God gives us what we seek. The man who is eager for acclaim for his good deeds gets it as he practices his public piety. The man who goes to church so that God will be appeased and will stay out of his affairs the other six days (or goes to church on Easter in the hope that God will not bother him the rest of the year!) will receive that boon (or bane) according to specification. The one who wants his morale boosted by a mild inoculation of religion will go home feeling better. *And the one who is truly seeking the Lord with all his heart will ever surely find Him!*

As the disciples set out for Galilee to meet Jesus where he had appointed, so for us right now there is a way to seek and find Him. The directions are clear enough, and handy to discover if you own a Bible or know where you can borrow one.

* * *

Students of the Greek text tell us that the Gospel of Mark ends abruptly at verse eight of chapter sixteen. The balance of the chapter was added later. There may be something suggestive for us about the ancient ending. The last three words of the authentic text read:

"they were afraid . . . ."

Well, naturally! Who is not tempted to be afraid as he comes out of bewilderment with the map of a brand new country in his hand, and the voice of command still ringing in his ears: "Think! . . . Check! . . . Talk! . . . Seek!"

There would be something wrong with anyone who would not be frightened, at least a little.

I do not remember being born, but I guess that like any other healthy, brand new human, I felt the spank and started to cry. So also with being born again into the new world of the risen Christ. The awakening can be a shock. But it is great to be alive!

Chapter VI

Living in the Light of Easter

"This was now the third time that Jesus was revealed to the disciples after he was raised from the dead."
— John 21:14

The irresistible summons which lifted His Only Begotten out of death and projected Him powerfully back into history was not a change of policy on the part of God with respect to His way of running the universe.

All of the miracles of the Bible, and most clearly in the case of those in which Jesus was involved, are presented to us without embarrassment as being entirely consistent with the nature of God and with His design for the creation. Miracles, as we become acclimated to them, do not introduce jarring notes into nature's symphony. They may surprise us at first by their unexpectedness, but with the whole composition in view, we can see that they belong. So Jesus, after the resurrection, points out to His followers who are finally ready to listen, that His dying and His rising again are the logical expression of what God has been saying all along about Himself in Scripture, and of what He has set out to do in human affairs.

The resurrection of Jesus was not a sudden change of divine policy, nor was the immediate situation much different, at least not in ways that contemporary news reporters might have noted. Tiberius Caesar still ruled at Rome, and Pontius Pilate governed in Judea. The Pharisees and Sadducees continued to quarrel over theology. Herod and his pals still dabbled in petty politics. The Jewish underground went on cooking up plots for the overthrow of Rome in Palestine; and ordinary folk went on doing what ordinary people do. The resurrection of Jesus apparently changed very little on the surface of life — no more, perhaps, than Easter Sunday is likely to change anything very much in our world.

What Jesus' resurrection did change both radically and rapidly was the way in which the disciples looked at the world, and the way they lived in the world from this point of time on. Once their Master had convinced them that He was indeed risen, their transformation was amazing to all who knew them. They had seen, as by a lightning flash, how deeply God had involved Himself on behalf of His people. This was for them now a different world altogether.

Christians today are meant to experience in their own lives, because Christ rose, something very like what happened to our first century spiritual forebears. ". . . If any man be in Christ, he is a new creature: old things are passed away; behold, all things are become new." This is Paul's way of describing what we have called, "Living in the Light of Easter."

There may be very different ways of arriving at such a life-changing experience. Some Christians report a burst of comprehension in a glad moment of time. For others it seems to be a process of enlightenment, almost imperceptible in its stages, over a period of years. Whichever way it occurs in your life or mine, there are at least two symptoms which help us to identify it. I find them epitomized in two incidents from the twenty-first chapter of John: the startling catch of fish, and Jesus' dialog with Peter. These suggest to me that living in the light of Easter will be living that is *Victorious* and *Vicarious*.

I. *Victorious Living*

The expression "Victorious Living" will be familiar to us if we have read at all widely in Christian devotional literature. If it tends to be limited in its use to any one segment of the church, that is too bad for it has a certain ring to it which challenges the dull, merely dutiful Christianity for which too many of us are willing to settle. Something a little more martial could be in order!

While the Bible is not the belligerent book that some of its critics accuse it of being, singling out passages from Joshua or certain of the Psalms or the Revelation, it does employ military metaphors frequently to describe the kind of life we ought to be enjoying as God's people. So do many of our favorite hymns, such as: "Onward Christian Soldiers," of course, and "Lead On O King Eternal," "Fight the Good Fight," or "A Mighty Fortress Is Our God." Some literalistic peace lovers have been heard to object to "militaristic" terminology in hymns, for the same reason probably that they disapprove of Sunday School lessons about what David did to Goliath. This is no place to get into the debate as to whether playing soldier, or cowboys and Indians, or cops and robbers is demoralizing for children. Some good child psychologists insist that tales of violence, from the Bible and elsewhere, constitute quite a wholesome diet for normal youngsters and leave no morbid after-effects, provided that the blood-and-thunder is dealt with in a matter-of-fact way. Milton Mayer, that brilliant, articulate leader in the work of the Society of Friends, has written a whimsical account of his efforts to detach his children from their toy sub-machine guns, and to dissuade them from rehearsing endless variations on TV gangster and cowboy-western slaughter scenes. In the end he gave up gracefully, deciding to wait a few years before trying to convert his offspring to his own pacifism.

By conviction (and I trust in practice too) a peace-maker, I nevertheless find it hard to go along with those who would force our great fighting hymns to check their weapons at the church door. I vaguely recall one such attempt which ended up with something like this:

> "Onward Christian brothers, working hard for peace;
> By non-violent methods, causing wars to cease."

— noble enough in intent, but taking the tingle out of a wonderful hymn we all love to sing (and, with the help of the right accompanist, to swing!) Rightly interpreted, there is nothing bloodthirsty about the military imagery of our hymns or about the concept of victorious living to be found in corresponding Biblical passages. What would anyone dare substitute for Paul's great "gladiator" sermon:

> "Stand therefore, having girded your loins with truth, and having put on the breastplate of righteousness; having your feet shod with the preparation of the gospel of peace (!); above all taking the shield of faith, . . . the helmet of salvation, and the sword of the Spirit, which is the word of God."

There ought to be something as thrilling as a cavalry charge in a church program. There should be exhilaration in a victory over temptation to compare with young David's toppling of Goliath!

On the other hand, if the term "Victorious Living" suggests only a piety that is mostly parading — far from the beachheads and foxholes of life, or uncommitted to the revolutionary Christian Causes of our time — it will be a travesty on the New Testament. Parades have their place for the raising of morale. They speak of power, enthusiasm, and anticipated triumph. The crowds in church for Easter Sunday can be a means of witnessing to the world that God is sovereign by those who belong to Him; that Christ is Lord of life and Conqueror of death. But parades without engagement can be an exercise in futility, as General McClellan demonstrated during the Civil War. Pageantry on the parade ground or in the church sanctuary may make the war seem won when it is scarcely begun. The Christian's warfare is not a romantic story of Sir Galahad in shining hardware, noisily routing all the villains within reach. There is a wry little parable perhaps in the fact that "Onward Christian Soldiers!" was written by an English clergyman for a group of children to help keep them in line on their way to a Sunday School rally in a neighboring village! In contrast, the mood of the Christian life is fairly grim at times and is probably more adequately reflected in Martin Luther's verses. He had a fearfully complicated task on his hands. He saw himself as a man fighting for his life in the thick of battle, but his eye was on the Captain of his salvation, and his war taunt was:

> "Let goods and kindred go; This mortal life also;
> The body they may kill: God's truth abideth still.
> His kingdom is forever!"

It is not that warlike words are the *only* way we can say it. The lives of most of us are not as dramatic as Luther's, although our times may be just as terrifying in some ways. It might be helpful if we could associate Victorious Living with a synonym more suggestive of the

normal tone of our existence. Would it be too prosaic to
substitute the very commonplace adjective "Successful?"
Living in the light of Easter may be thought of as Successful Living. The illustration Jesus chose for an object lesson
was of this character. Peter, James and John and the rest
were in boats on the Sea of Galilee. How better could they
relax after the emotionally exhausting days just past than
to return to familiar surroundings and to practice their
former profession for awhile? So they launched their
boat and started in to fish. It was relaxing enough at first
but increasingly frustrating for expert fishermen. They
were catching nothing. Then, just at dawn, Someone on
the shore was hallooing across the water:

"Any luck?"

"No!" they came back, not recognizing the voice, but
   being grateful for the courtesy.

"Then cast on the right side of the boat once more, and
   you will have fish!"

They did as they were told and now could not pull the
net in, so filled was it with large fish. In an instant they
sensed that this was the hand of God giving them a token
as they obeyed His word, that henceforth they would be
successful Christian men.

Can you conceive of anything more telling for Jesus to
have done for these men to fill them with new hope? The
context was that of everyday life. The miracle was spectac-
ular only as to its timing. They were in the well-known
place at the well-understood task when a quiet voice spoke
out of the unseen in plain words to their problem. What
they were directed to do may have sounded slightly unreasonable for a moment, especially to weary men who had
tried every fisherman's trick at least twice. But it was well
within their power to do what He suggested to them now.

This is the way God deals with us ordinarily, is it not?

He does not drop fish or dollar bills from the sky. He does not equip us with a magical abracadabra à la Arabian Nights, or require us to work ourselves up to worthiness with the technique of self-mortification practiced by Hindu holy men. We are given reasonable responsibility — to mend and manipulate our nets; to use our brains and spend our strength. If we will do our small share as men under orders to Jesus Christ, the promise is Success.

No need to leave ourselves the convenient evasion exit by which we sometimes hide from embarrassment when our prayers are not answered. It is true enough that God's standard of success will differ at times from ours. But when in the Psalms and in the Gospel and elsewhere, the Word of God promises to the obedient "Blessings" (another word for success in the Bible), it is not mocking us with paradox. God is not devious. He does not promise bread and give a stone. His answers are not ambiguous if we will hear Him out. The promises of God are not "Yea and Nay," but always "Yea"! (In Paul's quaint way of saying it, he means that God does not talk out of both sides of His mouth.) And He knows *how* to give good gifts unto His children. The Jesus who rose from the dead is the Jesus who for thirty years and more learned to look at human problems from the perspective of a human being. He tells us that God delights to give us cause for happiness.

In the light of this incident on Galilee, as well as from other post-resurrection promises acted and spoken and written, you and I have a perfect right to expect things to go well in our lives. That is, of course, if we are obeying. There may be ups and downs; moments of sadness as well as of joy; bright days and clouded ones. But God being sovereign, and God being involved with us and having brought that involvement into sharp focus by Jesus' dying and rising, there is only one logical outcome to be expected. If we trust and obey, we shall be happy with a deep and durable happiness. We may expect to taste the quiet thrill of victorious living or, to say it another way, to see a steadily unfolding pattern of success — like a picture being painted by a competent artist; like a structure gradually emerging from a set of blueprints; or like a crop coming into harvest-stage; or like a marvelous catch of fish! The method may be temporarily unclear, but we can know whom we have believed and can be persuaded that he will protect and multiply our investment all the way. "We know that all things work together for good, to them that love God." We know it through Jesus Christ crucified and risen. This is the stuff of Victorious Living. It is also the source of:

II. *Vicarious Living*

"Vicarious" is a second word which Christians should recognize on sight. If you read in theological literature, sooner or later it will turn up. It can turn up elsewhere, too. The word comes from the Latin where it is spelled almost the same way and means essentially "substituted." If we do not recall having seen the full nine-letter adjective, we may identify a part of it. A "vicar" is a deputy: a man who represents or takes the place of someone else in the performance of some function or task. You may learn that from your dictionary, theological reading aside. The word "vice" when hyphenated and used in an official title has the same import. A vice-president substitutes for the Big Boss when the latter is not around.

Jesus is said to have died vicariously. A person who dies vicariously is one who perishes voluntarily, or in spite of his wishes, for another's sake. Thus a soldier who deliberately stops a bullet intended for his buddy, or a secret service agent who is killed while protecting the man he has been assigned to guard, may be said to have been a vicarious victim. So also is a mother who might lose her life in snatching her baby from under the wheels of a truck; or a father drowned in the act of rescuing his son who could not swim. There are many noteworthy examples in literature and human history of vicarious dying. For Christians, the supreme and in many ways unique example is Jesus who died on the cross for us, both in the sense of being an innocent victim and in the more wonderful role of an atoning Saviour. Isaiah the prophet foretold His death, we believe, when he wrote:

> "He was wounded for our transgressions; he was bruised for our iniquities. The chastisement of our peace was upon him, and by his stripes we are healed."

And we sing gratefully:

"He died that we might be forgiven; He died to make us good,
That we might go at last to heaven, saved by His precious blood."

There is such a matter also as vicarious *living*. We speak in common experience of a vicarious thrill, by which we mean a sensation of pleasure or excitement which you and I may share because of something sensational that someone else has done while we were watching. The feeling you get with the score tied in the ninth inning, our side being up, when the team's weakest hitter lofts a home run, is vicarious! Seeing your son or daughter tapped for the Honor Society could provide another example.

It may be a vicarious joy, or sorrow, on Award Day. Perhaps your child is passed by, and it hurts you as much as him. Some of us have a hard time in hospital rooms listening to the story of gruesome operations. We feel vicarious pain or vicarious nausea. In medical terminology, incidentally, there are technical uses for this same interesting word. Perhaps, however, it is already sufficiently defined.

As Christians we can by this time begin to see that some form of vicarious living on our part is a right response to Jesus' vicarious dying. Do you know the gospel song that begins like this:

"I gave my life for thee; My precious blood was shed
  That thou might ransomed be, and quickened from the dead,"

and ends with the searching question which the reproachful Saviour is asking,

"I gave, I gave my life for thee
                What hast thou given for me?"

That is a good question. It can be fittingly answered in the words of another and greater hymn:

"Were the whole realm of nature mine
  That were a present far too small;
  Love, so amazing, so divine
  Demands my soul; my life; my all!"

Living in the light of Easter will be this kind of vicarious living. Paul puts it into another noble passage printed in our Bibles as prose although it sings like a poem:

"For the love of Christ constraineth us; because we thus judge,
  That if one died for all, then were all dead:
  And that he died for all, that they which live should not henceforth
  Live unto themselves,
  But unto him who died for them and rose again."

He goes on to describe the Christian as an Ambassador for Christ, a striking and suggestive idea with its connotation of *shared* authority, dignity, and power. But again, as with the military metaphor for victorious Christian living, this figure borrowed from international diplo-

macy may seem to us to be a far cry from the kind of
Christian career for which we are cut out. Famous
preachers, heroic missionaries, prophets and apostles —
these fit the ambassador analogy, but we seldom do. Can
we perhaps find a humbler illustration to fit our case?

We have one before us in Jesus' conversation with Peter
by the lake side.

I am grateful for John's report of what took place
after that huge catch of fish had been landed and break-
fast had been enjoyed. Jesus takes Peter aside and in
an exquisitely wise and gentle interview asks him three
times how matters stand between the two of them. Three
times Peter is given opportunity to affirm his loyalty to
the One he thrice denied before the dawn of the terrible
crucifixion day. And three times Jesus gives the same com-
mission to the broken man before Him, "Feed my lambs;
Feed my sheep; Feed my sheep."

Years later in his letter to the scattered churches, Peter
is passing on the same gracious task to his fellow pastors:

> "Feed the flock of God which is among you, taking the over-
> sight thereof, not by constraint, but willingly. . . . And when
> the chief Shepherd shall appear ye shall receive a crown of
> glory that fadeth not away."

The business of being a Pastor could be disheartening,
when one takes it seriously (and ruinous if one does not)!
What best keeps a man on the track, and of good courage,
is remembering that he is a vicar of Christ. This is His
church, and one works under His direction; His authority
is behind me, every time I preach, or visit a hospital room
or push a doorbell. One almost feels like an ambassador
at that!

Is it so different with the layman's role? Does the New
Testament anywhere distinguish between professionals and
amateurs as to our responsibility in living for the One who

died for us? I cannot recall any such distinction. On the contrary, whether you happen to be a salaried Christian worker, or an ordained Elder or Deacon, or a teacher in the Church School, or an officer in an organization, or just a run-of-the-mill member makes no difference. If you are a Christian according to the Scriptural doctrine of the priesthood of all believers, you are a vicar of Christ just as much as any clergymen you may wish to mention, and just as much as the Pope in Rome who likes to claim the vicar title as his very own. In fact, one suspects that a pope must have a rather hard time being a vicar of Christ, loaded down as his life is with so many complicated costumes and customs. I should think that they would get in his way when he tries to make Jesus' way plain to people. With him, I'm sure, as with all professional Christians, it is easy to get so bogged down in the mechanics of church business, and so distracted by management problems, that we are tempted to forget whom we represent and what He commanded us to do. I have an article in my file on the work of the pastor, written by a well-known minister, entitled "Can a Preacher Be Saved?"

In some ways it is easier for you to be Christ's vicar than it is for me!

This controversial question aside, however, every one of us like Peter is needing to be reminded three times a day at least, and often more, that the logic of an encounter with a crucified and risen Lord leads us straight into a life of service in His name. The idea that loving service is a virtue is not new. Some form of the Golden Rule, for instance, is as old as religion itself and is found in practically every religious tradition, not to mention the creeds of "service clubs." What is unique in the New Testament teaching, and what dawns upon us gloriously in the resurrection Gospel, is that *victorious living and vicarious living are two sides of the same truth.* Christ is risen; therefore, any one of us can serve successfully. The struggle to live for Him, and for others for His sake, can be pleasant because it is possible. Holiness *is* happiness. It actually is more blessed (successful!) to give than to receive. Calvin Laufer expresses it nicely in his discipleship hymn:

> "We've sought and found Thee in the secret place
> And marveled at the radiance of Thy face;
> But often in some far off Galilee
> Beheld Thee fairer yet while serving Thee.
>
> "We've seen Thy glory like a mantle spread
> O'er hill and dale in saffron flame and red;
> But in the eyes of men, redeemed and free,
> A splendor greater yet while serving Thee."
> — Copyright, Calvin W. Laufer, 1919

The wisdom and power of Almighty God, revealed in Jesus' rising from the dead, await channeling through your life and mine whenever we are ready to discard our apprehensions and to start showing our love for Jesus by living for others as He did.

Christian biography is full of testimonies of great heroes of the faith whose lives were defeated and unproductive until one day they decided to live in the light of the resurrection, for a change, and thereby gave God a chance to show what He could do with a person confidently yielded to His will.

The only completely convincing illustration that I know, though, is the one a Christian permits himself to have in his own life as he responds to the Word of God.

And I am particularly grateful today to John and his Gospel for this chapter in which Christ speaks to us through Peter, and makes so plain to him and to us, that living in the light of Easter is victorious and vicarious living, and that the two are, in essence, the very same.

Chapter VII

Something Wonderful
Something Terrible
Something Dreamed About,
and Something Seen

"As they were saying this, Jesus himself stood among them. But they were startled and frightened, and supposed that they saw a spirit. And he said to them, 'Why are you troubled, and why do questionings rise in your hearts? See my hands and my feet, that it is I myself; handle me, and see; for a spirit has not flesh and bones as you see that I have.' And while they still disbelieved for joy, and wondered, he said to them, 'Have you anything here to eat?' They gave him a piece of broiled fish, and he took it and ate before them. Then he said to them, 'These are my words which I spoke to you, while I was still with you, that everything written about me in the law of Moses and the prophets and psalms must be ful-

*filled.' Then he opened their minds to understand the
scriptures, and said to them, 'Thus it is written, that the
Christ should suffer and on the third day rise from the
dead, and that repentance and forgiveness of sins should
be preached in his name to all nations, beginning from
Jerusalem. You are witnesses of these things."*

— Luke 24:36-48

(The improbable title, to say nothing of the style and content of this sermon, calls for a preliminary word of explanation.
It was prepared for delivery in a village church in Vermont
on an Easter Sunday when, because of schedule pressures, the
Church School was canceled. The curriculum had called for
the quarter's study to climax with a lesson on the resurrection.
Instead, the lesson was omitted and the children were encouraged to attend one of the church services with their
parents. Having been forewarned, the preacher resolved to
use the ploy indicated below. Incidentally, very much the
same material with some adaptation was preached one Easter
afternoon to a congregation in the Lancaster, Pennsylvania
County Jail. They seemed to enter into the spirit of it.)

I am afraid that we shall not be able to have a sermon
after all! You see there was no time for our Sunday School
lesson today. We are so crowded for space and time on
Easter Sunday, and there is very much to distract: the
arranging of flowers, the extra choir rehearsal, the ones
who come early for a good seat, the new dresses and hats
and suits and ties, and all the joyful excitement in the air!

But we should at least have a Sunday School lesson, even
if we must shift it to church time — especially this year,
because since Christmas we have been studying the life
of Jesus and spending a Sunday on each of the high spots
in His life. The highest spot of all is Easter, the day of
His rising from the dead; the day of His victory over the
worst that man could do to Him when He showed that
He was the Son of God with power, as the Bible puts it.

So this morning instead of a sermon, we are going to have our Sunday School lesson after all. I want to speak not to the philosophers and scholars in the congregation, but to "children." I trust that those of you who came expecting something all dressed up to fit into the style parade will be patient, and perhaps even listen a little!

As the church bulletin says, I want to talk about "Something Wonderful, Something Terrible, Something Dreamed About and Something Seen."

1. The Something Wonderful Is Life, and Especially Human Life

Put your finger on that spot on your wrist that flickers while you watch it. Feel the gentle "thump, thump, thump." It is your pulse, the echo of your heart beat. Try to stop it for a minute or so, the way you can hold your breath. You can't. And you didn't start it going either. It began weeks and weeks before you were even born. When you were tiny and still didn't know anything or think of anything, there it was at work — thump, thump, thumping away. You were alive, for your heartbeat is the whisper of that wonderful something called life.

Here is an object I brought from home for you to see. What is it? That's right — a microscope. There was a time when you were so small that you could not possibly be seen except with this. You were hidden away in your mother's body no bigger than the point of a pin. Yet you were all there — not the fifty, sixty, or one-hundred pounds of you now — but the pattern of you was there, and that wonderful pattern told everything important about the body that was going to be yours; every special feature that makes you *You.* Before you were as big as a bean, there was the plan which said whether you were to be a boy or a girl, with brown eyes or blue, tall or short, looking like Mother or Dad or a bit of both. All of these were ready before you were born, and very much else besides. All you needed to do was to breathe and eat and exercise and grow, and as you did, everything fell into its proper place just the way cows head for their right stalls or children find their own desks in school.

More wonderful yet is the fact that you are not only alive and planned, but that you are a *human* being. All we have said so far is as true of your pet dog or cat as it is of you. But human life is much more wonderful because it is life that can think about itself and plan for itself and make up its own mind and discover the meanings in the whole wide world around it. Everywhere you look, in houses and schools and churches, at autos and planes and rifles and cash-registers, in books and magazines and TV sets and Bibles, you can see what human beings can make. When you look into the mirror and think to yourself, "Hi, there!" you are doing something which no one but a human, living creature can do, even though puppy dogs and parakeets act almost as if they could talk matters over with themselves in the mirror. (Actually you and I do not need mirrors to help us talk with ourselves, and as we get older and do not hear other people so well, we will be talking to ourselves more and more!) But perhaps we have said enough to start the idea simmering. What a wonderful thing is life — human life especially! How fortunate we are to be alive, and to be able to do things with our lives that are useful and interesting: to work with our bodies and our minds. Do you not agree?

2. *The Something Terrible Is Death, and Especially Human Death*

Last week we took our Christmas tree to the dump and threw it over the bank. In some less wintry places the snow goes off earlier and they get rid of Christmas trees sooner, but our Vermont holidays seem to run together! Anyway, the tree was dead and dry and ugly, and when you moved it the needles fell off. It had been dead three months or more. It stopped growing one snowy day last December when the children and I hiked up the hill behind Bradley's barn and cut it for 25¢ cash. It did not look dead for awhile, but it was. It was dead just like these beautiful Easter flowers here today. The cut ones are all dead. In a few days they will turn brown and smell bad, and we shall have to throw them away, too. I am sorry, but I am trying to remind you of the fact that all living things must die.

Now probably when an Easter lily dies, nobody will weep. Flowers, new ones, are fairly easy to get where these were bought. Especially as spring comes we expect to see flowers almost everywhere we look. But some forms of life are "higher," we say, and harder to replace, and therefore more precious. We had a dog, Teddy, when I was small, and a loveable pup he was. He had a fondness for fresh paint, however, and in the end it killed him. I can remember how the whole family cried when we found him, except perhaps for Uncle Ernest who was not very tender-hearted about dogs. We planned a funeral service for Teddy; we found a gravestone made out of a board; and Uncle Ernest suggested that we bury him under the grapevine because then his death "would not be in vain," he said. It was a sad moment! I remember that I cried more than the others. Dogs like Teddy are hard to find, I thought. Perhaps not, but it was the way I felt at the time.

I do know, and all of us realize this, that when people die it is much worse, because worthwhile human beings are much more precious than any animal, even the most expensive one. People whom we love can never really be replaced when we lose them by death. When a man with a sick mind shot Abraham Lincoln, the whole country mourned because men like Lincoln are not born more than once in a hundred or a thousand years, and men like that were greatly needed just at that time in America. The more we appreciate how precious human life is, the more plain it becomes, when we let ourselves think about it, that human death is terrible as well as sad. It is worse than having your house burn down; worse than being robbed of all your money; worse than breaking your arm or leg and having to go to the hospital. It is worse than having to go to jail.

We are not supposed to spend all our time thinking about dying, but it certainly is a sensible thing to remember that all living things must die, and that includes people. It includes you and me. And because life is wonderful, death is terrible. I do not mean the dying itself; that can be quite comfortable, I have heard, and even a relief when you are old and sick and tired. I mean the whole idea of dying is a great big disappointment to something inside us which wants to go on living, and growing, and learning. But our bodies, like any other living thing, start dying almost as soon as we are alive. For awhile life is stronger and wins the fight with sickness and with pain and weakness. But after a few years death begins to catch up and conquer; so that people slow down and start to puff when they climb stairs; they need stronger glasses and find it hard to stand up straight and all the rest of growing old. Some folks talk tenderly about death as if it were a friend in disguise. "Come, sweet death!" wrote one famous poet, but maybe he was just pretending to like it.

The Bible calls death by the name of Enemy. Our own

feelings talk that way, too. Did you ever stumble over a dead animal in the field, or in the woods? Remember how it made you shiver? When Jesus, who saw everything in the world exactly as it truly is, got close to death, He shuddered too, although He was very brave. He knew that if it could, death would wipe out the whole human race and turn this beautiful world into a desert. That is why we call it terrible.

3. *The Something Dreamed About Is a Life after Death*

One way men have tried to get away from thoughts about the terribleness of death has been to dream about another life ahead for which death turns out to be the doorway. American Indians dreamed about a Happy Hunting Ground where they could take one arrow-shot at a fat ten point buck and hit it any time they tried. The Greeks and Romans, Egyptians and Babylonians; black men and brown men, red men and yellow men and white men; people in cold countries and hot, in crowded cities and on lonely farms — all kinds of people have always dreamed about a life where death will be no more, where there will be no pain, nor hunger and thirst, nor loneliness or grief, neither death nor any of its ugly grandchildren.

These dreamers saw some things happening which made them hopeful. Springtime was one, when trees that looked dead came to life. Seed was another, so dry and lifeless to look at until you put it into the warm, moist earth where it could sprout. There was the caterpillar, too, crawling to some safe spot, winding himself up in his cocoon and falling asleep to wake up at last as a butterfly. Then there were the pictures which passed through men's thoughts while they slept, especially dreams about dead people. Someone who had died would seem to visit them while they were dreaming — maybe a long gone grandfather, or a son who had been killed in war, always trying to say something and suddenly gone when a noise awakened the sleeper. Such happenings made men hopeful that something lay ahead of them after death.

Most of all, I suppose, it was that inner voice we call instinct which gave them hope. It makes no noise, but we hear it whisper just the same. Birds must hear some such voice that tells them when and where to fly when winter comes. It tells a newborn calf that there is something for him to drink nearby, and where to look for it, and how to suck and swallow. It must be instinct that lets the caterpillar know when cocoon time comes, and shows him how to spin the threads round and round himself.

Human beings have instincts, too, to protect them from danger and to teach them how to live with one another. Our instincts are very strong. One of them is what we have just been talking about: an inner voice which says hopefully, "Death is not the end. It does not have the last word. There is another life waiting for you if you will learn to please God!"

But in days gone by there was no proof. It was like a dream, and one did not know whether to believe that silent whisper or not. No one ever came back in flesh and blood with souvenirs of the distant country beyond death, proofs such as Columbus brought back from the new land he had discovered. That is, nobody came back until Jesus rose from the dead on the first Easter and showed His disciples His new, glorious body with strange new powers. He promised them that if they only believed in Him, they, too, could have such a body and the everlasting life that man has always dreamed about, because their enemy, death, had been overcome.

4. *The Something Seen, Therefore, Was Jesus after He Had Risen from the Dead*

Jesus' resurrection was no dream. The disciples thought it might be, at first. Earliest at the sepulchre where he had been buried, were some women who had a vision of angels saying to them, "He is not here, for He is risen. Come, see the place where the Lord lay!" To the rest of the disciples, their words seemed to be idle tales and very difficult to believe. Peter and John ran to the tomb, and they too found it empty. And still it all seemed unreal.

So it seemed to two disciples who set out along the road leading from Jerusalem, where Jesus had been crucified, to a village called Emmaus. As they were walking Jesus Himself drew near and went with them. Their eyes were kept from recognizing Him as He talked to them about the promises in the Bible concerning Christ's death and resurrection. However, before the journey to Emmaus was over, these two men were certain that the mysterious Stranger who had joined them in their journey was none other than their Lord Jesus whom they supposed they had lost altogether and would never see again.

We might still think, as did some of the doubtful friends of Jesus when they heard about the walk to Emmaus, that these scattered surprises were the stuff that dreams are made of. But the story of what they saw does not stop there. Listen! The disciples were together in a favorite meeting place, listening to Peter who also said that he had seen the Lord alive.

More proof was piling up fast. Too many people were seeing the same thing in too many different places for it to be called foolishness. So they chattered and shivered and hoped that they all would get a glimpse of what was happening, but they could not help feeling frightened when they thought about it. It was like being in a

haunted house and waiting for ghosts. Then all at once
(this is how the Bible tells it):

> "As they were saying this, Jesus himself stood among them.
> But they were startled and frightened, and supposed that they
> saw a spirit. And he said to them, 'Why are you troubled, and
> why do questionings rise in your hearts? See my hands and
> my feet, that it is I myself; handle me, and see; for a spirit
> has not flesh and bones as you see that I have.' And while
> they still disbelieved for joy, and wondered, he said to them,
> 'Have you anything here to eat?' They gave him a piece of
> broiled fish, and he took it and ate before them."

Ghosts do not eat fish and leave crumbs. This was no
dream!

For forty days Jesus stayed with His friends, teaching
them from the Scriptures, explaining the meaning of His
life and death and resurrection, and then telling them
goodbye but promising to be with them always, through
the one we call the Holy Spirit, until the end of time.
So they went everywhere, preaching the good news and
teaching the meaning of what they themselves had
learned, and sharing the same promise of Life Forever
which Jesus had given to them. "It is for everyone," they
said, "everyone who will trust in Jesus as the Savior and
obey Him as the Lord."

They knew it was no dream. They had seen Him, and
they were so positive of it that they faced death and
troubles gladly, singing hymns of victory since death now
had no power to destroy them. It could only shove them
farther along toward heaven. "That which we have seen
and heard we declare to you," they said. And they were
good and honest men who could be depended on to tell
the truth.

This is how the story of the life of Jesus here on earth
ends. And this is how a person's strong, sure hope of life
after death begins. Now we know that wonderful as life

is, eternal life is better yet; terrible as death is, Jesus Christ has conquered it. The happiness that men always and everywhere have dreamed about is what the disciples of Jesus discovered when they saw Him in His resurrection body. They help us to discover it, too, with our minds, as we listen to their story. And someday we shall see Jesus, as Paul the great apostle reminds us, "face to face."

There still are many, many people in this world who have no sureness about eternal life — only the dream. They try not to think of death. Or they pretend to themselves that it is no worse for a man to die than for a Christmas tree, an Easter lily, or a pet dog.

How foolish and how sad it is not to pay attention to Jesus, or to those who knew Him and saw the whole thing happen! How much more sensible it is to trust Him than to doubt; how much more joyful to discover what He has to give us than just to dream!

Chapter VIII

The Body That Shall Be

*"But some one will ask, 'How are the dead raised?
With what kind of body do they come?'"*
— I Corinthians 15:35

Christians of the first century did not debate the resurrection of Jesus. They simply declared it. It was the only adequate explanation for the existence of the Christian church. Had there been no resurrection, there would have been no church. It was as simple to them as that. To have introduced the question whether it really happened, among members of one of those early churches, would have been like attending, in our own day, a meeting of the stockholders of General Motors and raising one's hand to ask whether the gasoline motor is likely to prove feasible for use in transportation. Presumably the existence of G.M. is an adequate answer to such a silly question!

Principal J. S. Whale of Cambridge University, who is not given to rash remarks, offers this verdict:

> "To say that God revealed himself in Jesus, or that God was in Christ reconciling the world, is to say nothing of real meaning unless we take our stand with the New Testament at one decisive point. That point is where God manifested Jesus as the Son of God with power by the resurrection from the dead."

He continues:

> "All the evidence of the New Testament goes to show that the burden of the good news or gospel was not 'Follow this Teacher and do your best,' but Jesus and the Resurrection. You cannot take that away from Christianity without radically altering its character and destroying its very identity."
>
> — *Christian Doctrine,* 1941, p. 69

To be sure, Christians of the first century had an advantage over us which Paul points up in the early verses of his great essay on the subject found in I Corinthians 15. He reminds his readers that at the date of his writing there were many still alive who had been with Jesus during the forty days between His resurrection and His ascension to the Father. If one had sincere doubts, he could go and listen firsthand to a thoroughly trustworthy man telling what he had seen and heard. Yet, so in a sense can we, for we are quite sure now — after decades of careful critical scholarship — that we have in our New Testament the authentic testimony of these same witnesses. And it is apparent that all of them consider the resurrection of Jesus Christ to be axiomatic; not to be argued but affirmed. His resurrection is the reason for the existence of the church.

Conceivably, it may take us a bit more time to study the evidences with the help of books than it used to take some to travel, say, from Rome to Jerusalem in order to talk to James, the Lord's brother, or His mother Mary, or Simon Peter. If a good library is nearby, it could take less time. Either way, the outcome can be just as reassuring. Here is what one, who is probably the most literate living authority on such evidence, has to say:

> "I do not want to be sarcastic, or mention anything of a fantastic nature, but after looking at this problem myself for about 30 years, I have about come to believe that theories which attempt to explain away the faith of the early church in the bodily resurrection of Christ are about as foolish as the theory held by a few strange persons in this world — that the earth is flat. . . . The author now in middle life with perhaps not more than a quarter-century yet to live, cannot afford to take time to read a book attempting to set forth the foolish idea that the earth is flat — or to read, study and ponder every new work that comes from a rationalist's brain that refuses to give honest, full, deserved consideration to this stupendous miracle which has moved the world, established the church, destroyed paganism, quickened the life of millions, and proved a light that no wind of infidelity has ever been able to distinguish."
>
> — Wilbur M. Smith, *Therefore Stand!*
> W. A. Wilde Co., 1945, p. 406

What interests Paul more, however, than debating the resurrection of Jesus is explaining the practical bearing it has upon a person's thinking and living. As we read the great Apostle's words on this subject in his Corinthian letter, we discover that the main part of his presentation deals with the way in which the destiny of the entire human race depends upon the resurrection fact. God is not at the mercy of what He has made; He is in charge. We are not wasting our time being men of good will. Every drop of blood, of sweat, of tears shed for Christ's sake is an investment in treasure which will not rot; in security that does not rest upon any human government or economic system; in life more abundant and eternal. If Christ had not risen, we Christians would be of all men most pitiable with our fond delusions. But now we are the darlings of destiny. This is Paul's thesis through verse 34.

Then he pauses as he thinks of his audience in Corinth and asks: "Any questions?"

Right away, being an author who knows to keep in rapport with his readers, he overhears what the questions will be, questions such as: "How literally are we supposed to take the life to come? How personally do we share in it? Dare we expect to meet our loved ones there? Will we recognize them? What will we look like?" Paul listens in imagination to these crowding questions, and then he starts to set down what we have before us in our Bibles as verses 35 to 53. "Your questions," he is saying, "boil down to two:

    1st. How are the dead raised? and
    2nd. With what body do they come?"

Let us consider what he has to say in that order.

1. *How Are the Dead Raised?*

The exact intent of this question is not quite clear in the English phrase. What is being asked for, one gathers from Paul's answer, is not a scientific description of the process involved. Neither Paul's reading public then, nor any of us today, can know enough about the nature and behavior of matter to be ready for an explanation of the transmutation of organisms from corruptible to incorruptible existence. We should remind ourselves often that the reason the Bible does not talk like a scientific textbook is not that God does not know as much as twentieth century scientists about the universe or the atom or the human mechanism. It just means that He knows *so much more* than any generation of scientific men that communication is a problem. It is like having a contemporary nuclear physicist on the faculty of First Presbyterian

Kindergarten. "Dr. Cranial, we have three levels in our school. There are the 3-year olds, the 4-year olds, and the pre-schoolers aged 5. I suppose if you are going to lecture on the quantum theory, you would prefer to address the latter?" I can hear the great man countering: "Do you mind if I show them a couple of sleight-of-hand tricks and then tell them about my latest visit to the zoo?"

God's Word discusses creation, and salvation and resurrection in very simple terms because you and I are just not yet smart enough, or mature enough, to go any deeper. Of course, 5-year olds feel much, much wiser than 3-year olds! And twentieth century scholars undeniably are way ahead of their first century counterparts in some ways. But it is still relative.

Paul treats the question, "How are the dead raised?" as an inquiry mainly concerned with the reasonableness or sensibleness of the resurrection concept. It is an approach very like the one Nicodemus made, you recall, in his interview with Jesus, who had said that to enter the Kingdom of God one must be born again. "How," persists Nicodemus, "can a man be born when he is old?" In other words, his was the old question about the practicability of teaching an old dog new tricks. Do people actually change by conversion for the better? So here.

"Is not the resurrection concept inherently illogical? One could accept the proposition that in order to show Himself in sovereign control of every situation and to vindicate His own honor, God might perform the unprecedented miracle of raising Jesus from the dead. But what warrant have we for expecting God to offer the same trip to thousands, nay millions, of ordinary run-of-the-mill Christians like us? Not that we doubt immortality. We have intimations of that. But the theory of resurrection, of bodies coming back to life, is much more radical

and less comfortable to contemplate." Such is the stumb-
ling-block for most of us, philosophy professors or plumb-
ers, when the New Testament talks as it does of life after
death. Resurrection sounds so unnatural and, frankly, so
unnecessary!

"Unnatural?" Paul is asking. "Take a simple illustration
from nature itself. Consider a seed. Observe its life cycle.
It appears on a plant as a part of a blossom. It ripens and
dries up and drops to the ground and is buried, and its
existence as a seed terminates. But we have learned to spell
that word with a "g." Its death is not terminal, but
germinal. The burial is the first stage of its new birth, no
longer to be a seed but as a plant — of wheat or of some
other grain."

A good analogy, Paul. An excellent illustration! At
Easter time we may even overwork it and imply that it
proves the resurrection. "I believe in the life to come,"
says the poet, "because of the argument of spring — the
budding trees; bulbs piercing the ground and aiming
green spears toward the sky; wheat lining up in rows as
the warm rain calls the roll." But these phenomena do not
prove that you and I will live again; still less that we shall
have new bodies. They merely illustrate that if we believe
in the resurrection of the body, we are not demanding that
our minds entertain an idea which is intrinsically ridicu-
lous or contrary to nature. With sufficient perspective the
terminal is seen to be germinal. Then, what looks like
oblivion when we lay it into a casket or lower it into a
grave may be, instead, the opening of the doorway to a
marvelous new dimension of existence. This is Paul's parable of the seed.

He goes further in his answer and we can follow. When
we speak of the resurrection of the body, let us not be
severely limited by what the word "body" ordinarily con-

notes. What it means on the seed-side of the dividing line, and what it means from the plant point of view are two quite different things. The trouble we have with "bodily resurrection" is a visual difficulty, like the one we have with "a personal God." The only persons we have ever seen are human beings, so the natural inference about a personal God is that He must be thought of as an extremely large, awfully ancient Man. But according to the Bible there are varieties of persons in God's universe. Take angels for a case in point. (Why do people accept so casually the likelihood of men from Mars or from some other habitable spot in some other solar system, and yet squirm and blush when the Bible talks about angels? Do we still insist that only Man could possibly emerge in the universe as a true person?)

But let us go back to the subject of unfamiliar bodies. If caterpillars were cynical, they would probably look scornful when informed about butterflies. If seeds were self-conscious and erudite and were resolved to compose a dictionary, they might set out to define "body" something like this:

> "BODY: a small, hard substance which develops in plant blossoms and fruit. Bodies come in various shapes and sizes but are usually spherical or egg-shaped. Some scholars propose that plants come from seeds and constitute an after-life stage of seed existence, hence that plants also deserve to be called "bodies," but to our knowledge no seed has ever lived through such a transition and come back to tell about it!"

After all, it takes considerable imagination even for us humans to conceive of a body prepared for us beyond, which is just as real yet as different in quality as a plant from its seed. But by looking at the seed-plant progression, or that of the caterpillar-butterfly, we are encouraged to concede that our bodies might actually be improved on in the state of eternity, even though they deteriorate in the process of time!

At this point we are perhaps ready for a third suggestion from Paul's analogy, namely, the reasonableness of believing in the persistence of our personal identity. "To every seed its own body . . ." is his way of expressing it.

I am afraid that our near-sighted, dubious peering into the grave, and our acquiescence in the ancient proverb about, "Ashes to ashes and dust to dust," may leave us, as we turn away from funerals, with the impression that the entrance of mankind into the life to come involves a kind of vast homogenization and absorption into the elemental universe. Certain of the religions of man seem to settle rather contentedly for that kind of immortality. One just gets lost in the crowd forever and ever.

There is a certain comfort, at times, in losing oneself in a crowd. When we are tired of taking responsibility, or of hearing the phone ring; when we have made an embarrassing mistake or done something illegal; for awhile we would prefer not to be picked out by a spotlight or to hear our name mentioned over the public address system. Normally, though, we enjoy the sound of our own names. Normally we like to think of ourselves as individuals, not just cogs in cosmic machinery. And normally, when we consider the life to come, we favor thinking of ourselves as plainly recognizable to ourselves and to others. When we must lose someone dear to us, we do not find it pleasant to imagine him de-personalized and dissolved into the whole. Frankly, there are a lot of people from the recent or distant past whom we should love to see again.

Right now, whether or not we realize it, we are speaking as if we wanted to believe for sure in the resurrection of the *body*, because anything remotely like human personality calls for a body of some sort — visible and material — for its self-expression.

We have been asking a very real and important question. Will we persist as individuals in spite of the brand new, and in some ways very different, body which is in the works for us? The New Testament answer *via* Paul and others is, "Yes!" God does not think merely in terms of masses; He thinks just as readily of particles. He does not prefer stereotype; He enjoys variety. Snowflakes and flowers, animals, birds, insects and fishes — there are no duplicates. Particularity is the rule. "To every seed its own body," even when the wheatfield covers a thousand acres or so and looks from a distance like one great uniform golden carpet. This is an element of God's greatness, His concern for the individual in plant or person.

"How are the dead raised? How can such a thing be?" This is question number one. And Paul's answer is along such a path as we have been following. We can hold this great hope just because God is the kind of worker that nature reveals Him to be.

2. With What Body Do They Come?

The second question is not quite the same as the first. The first is a question of principle: Are reasonable people permitted to believe in the bodily resurrection, or is it more sensible to settle for the immortality of the soul? But now we come to a question based more on curiosity. "What will we look like? What kind of body will we have, to correspond with such a change from seed to plant as has been in view?"

Curiosity is natural to the human mind, and to ask questions is not sinful. But God does not always answer our questions in exactly the way we might wish, any more than He does our prayers. Unlike a fortune-teller, much as we might like to have it so, He does not profess to deal in intriguing details about tomorrow or twenty years from now or beyond death's veil. He knows that we are not yet old enough to grasp the full range of His purpose for us. Yet He is not sourly uncommunicative. He is prepared to drop a cheering hint or two for those who are willing to ponder His Word in the gospel.

"*As in Adam all die, even so in Christ shall all be made alive.*" Here is the main clue to what the resurrection body will be like. We enter this life in the likeness of Adam; we are to inherit in That Life a likeness of the risen Christ. We have Him as our elder brother to show us what adult existence is intended to be like. John is saying much the same in his epistle:

> "Beloved, now are we the sons of God, and it doth not yet appear what we shall be: but we know that when he shall appear, we shall be *like him;* for we shall see him as he is" (I John 3:2).

If we think back to the accounts of Jesus' resurrection appearances — the fact that He was definitely Himself though not always immediately recognizable; that there was easy communication as He talked with them; that there was recollection of times past and of experiences together; that there was affection and the invitation for Peter and the rest to keep on loving Him — all this is unspeakably comforting. The old relationships still held good! But besides all that was familiar, there were the strange new powers — for instance, the ability to ignore locked doors, just as there had been to pass through the tightly sealed opening of the tomb. So when the moment came for Him to leave them, He could step back into invisibility across the boundary line between time and eternity as easily as you and I move from one room to another.

"There is a spiritual body," Paul explains. The word is *pneumatikos*, and the implication is exhilarating. Such a wonderful, powerful, spiritually obedient body as Jesus displayed briefly among His disciples is the closest, surely, that we can come to understanding what our own resurrection will involve. But in the passage before us, Paul points up three details which we have time today only to mention. He says,

A. *"It is sown in corruption, it is raised in incorruption."* His use of the word "corruption" is biological, not moral. The body which is planted like a seed in the ground, no matter how skilfully the embalmer's art may disguise or arrest the process, is disintegrating. This is a part of the wisdom of nature's cycle which encompasses all living things from the simplest to the most complex. Birth, nourishment, growth, aging, death — the continual merry-go-round of earth's biology looks to the natural man like the whole story. Yet, the prophets of religion and man's own instincts have insisted that the cycle is escapable, if only at the sad cost of losing our bodies, and the soul's taking flight bird-like from its cage.

Yet, while the thought of escape may sound good at first in certain unpleasant life-situations, for healthy-minded humans death is more a being banished from one's home and fatherland. Must we be disembodied spirits forever and ever when we die? "No!" says Scripture. We escape from this perishable dwelling into another, not made with hands, eternal, incorruptible and delightful. Our mortality is swallowed up by life. This is our biological expectation.

B. *"It is sown in dishonor, it is raised in glory."* Here Paul speaks morally. There is nothing dishonorable about death in nature. Everybody has to die, saints and sinners, the civilized and the savage; there are no natural exceptions. Conceivably, without any hope of another existence, a man's dying might be as dignified and as constructive an ending of his story as the harvesting of a crop of grain, or as the majestic toppling of a tree to become the humus for a new generation of saplings.

But, Paul reminds us, "the sting of death is sin!" Man does not die with a feeling of having fulfilled his destiny. He dies, if he dies alert, with a deep sense of frustration. No eulogy can do full justice to his situation. The only accurate comment on the best of men is that he has done much that he ought not to have done and has left undone much that he ought to have done, and his health as a person is very partial. At least these would be appropriate words at the funeral of anyone I have known, were there not the gospel which tells us that, "There is now no condemnation to them that are in Christ Jesus!"

The sting of death is indeed sin; and the strength of sin's claim against us is the acknowledged moral law, but "Thanks be to God who has given us the victory through our Lord Jesus Christ!" This is our dignity in dying.

"Brother Donkey," was the quaint, reproachful name given by an ancient saint to his body — so serviceable at times and so stubbornly rebellious at others. Well, Brother Donkey is going to become a glorious winged-horse (speaking morally, not biologically!) to carry our best ideals to a glad fulfillment. Would it not be a relief to have a body which found its delight in doing right, always? Like Jesus', for instance! Such is the prospect for those who identify their lives with His.

C. *"It is sown in weakness, it is raised in power."* Paul has pictured the resurrection body as biologically immortal and morally cooperative. Now here, I think, he is proposing that it will be mechanically skillful beyond anything we can presently imagine. It would be strange, do you not agree, if God were to give our souls these marvelous physical mechanisms called bodies in which to go to school on earth, and then had nothing corresponding for our spirits to use after graduation!

I sense that we live in a time when we can appreciate as never before how much more there is for our brains to grasp, our hands to manufacture, and our bodies to explore in this vast universe than earth-bound, oxygen-dependent, short-lived man can even begin to attend to. Furthermore, are we to believe that we mid-twentieth-century humans deserve to be the only ones to unlock the kind of secrets of time and space and energy which are tumbling open about us with such incredible rapidity? No, what we have just begun to taste of space-conquest, of electronic and atomic power, of the understanding of biochemistry and astrophysics belongs in all fairness to the entire human race from Adam onward!

I want to live to see what is coming; and if I understand the implications of the resurrection doctrine, I shall, though not by virtue of the body I have now, or the brain, or the limited life-span. We are seeing only the bare edge of an unexplored wilderness of wonders. How exciting to be able to believe that what is in store is not only deathlessness, and joyful holiness, but the fulfillment of man's instinctive longing to share in God's dominion over all creation — that career for which, as far back as racial memory can take us, man has believed himself ultimately to have been made!

We impoverish ourselves immeasurably if we close our mouths at that point in the Apostles' Creed where it bids us confess our belief in the resurrection of the body and the life everlasting. These phrases conjure up a prospect which is neither grotesque nor vague nor by any measurement theologically dull. The whole conception is reasonable, specific, and thrilling.

But let us remember that what we have been glimpsing is contingent on the substance of the gospel as a whole, and upon our acceptance of it in the person of the Lord Jesus Christ who is our Hope.

According to our lights (and on Easter Day in this place of Christian worship, visibility should be fairly good!) we must put our trust in Him who is the resurrection and the life. Otherwise, at the day of reckoning He may be forced by our unwillingness, to say to us, "Depart. I know you not."

He tells us tenderly but with utter honesty that the alternative to what we have had in view is "darkness, and weeping, and the gnashing of teeth."

Chapter IX

The Whereabouts
of our Risen Lord

(A Resurrection Postscript)

*"And when he had said this, as they were looking on,
he was lifted up, and a cloud took him out of their sight."*
— Acts 1:9

A non-believer, probing for soft spots in the Christian's
creed, might congratulate himself upon having found a
specially vulnerable one at this point in the Book of the
Acts. "Do you mean to tell me that Jesus took off vertically,
like a helicopter, while His disciples gaped and craned
their necks?" Could anything be more incredible to
modern man than such a picture, or harder to defend
against his cynicism? The doctrine of Christ's resurrection imposes no small strain on one's credulity. The story
of an exit like this could be the last straw!

To be sure, a lot of sensible matters can be made to sound
ludicrous if you let a scoffer invest them with his own

irreverent impressions. Any Christian doctrine can be
caricatured, and so made to sound indefensible. But let
the Bible itself tell the story quietly, simply, and in
context. Then let the reader ponder what is at stake. (A
book like C. S. Lewis' *Miracles* could help to rid us of
our prejudice against all Divine intervention in the affairs
of nature.) Once we have reached the place where we can
grant the New Testament its two main theses: First, that
Jesus was God incarnate, and Second, that having died
for our sins according to the Scriptures, He was raised
again the third day according to the Scriptures, then the
way described in the Book of Acts of getting Him back
home to His Father may turn out to be as appropriate as
any other we might invent.

"A cloud received him out of their sight." Consider the
fitness of what that said to those who watched. A luminous cloud is a favorite Biblical symbol of God's presence
among His people. During the wilderness journey from
Egypt; then at Mt. Sinai for the giving of the Law; again
when Solomon was ready to dedicate the temple at Jerusalem — each time God manifested Himself in a cloud.

When Jesus is baptized, and later when He is trans-
figured on the mountaintop in Caesarea, God attests His
Son's authority, speaking from a hovering cloud: "This is
my beloved. Heed him!"

How more perfectly could it be made memorable to a
company of Jews, steeped in Scripture symbolism, that
Jesus was returning to His Divine existence, than by His
stepping from them into a waiting cloud?

Clouds have two natural messages for me, which Scripture reinforces. They can speak of majesty. Few sights are
more awe-inspiring than a tremendous bank of "thunder-
heads," as the farmer calls them, cumulus clouds, stacked
up against a deep blue summer sky. Or recall other forma-

tions as sunset, aflame with colors no artist could ever fully reproduce. How gloriously they suggest the majesty of God and the might of our exalted Savior. "Behold, he cometh in the clouds, and every eye shall see him!"

Again, one may stand in mountain mist or ocean fog and feel enclosed and somehow permeated by the gentle mystery of moisture. God, too, is "closer than breathing; nearer than hands or feet," and Jesus by virtue of His partaking of the Divine nature can be with us always.

We are proposing that in the cloud imagery which Jesus exploits as His means of departing is to be found a clear lesson as to His whereabouts. It speaks of His exaltation and of His nearness, corresponding nicely to what theologians call the "transcendence" and the "immanence" of God. We start with the latter quality and say that:

1. *We Are to Be Conscious of Jesus' Nearness*

"He ascended into heaven . . ." affirms the Apostles' Creed. Of course, if you insist on holding to a juvenile, Jack-and-the-Beanstalk mental picture about heaven, then modern scientifically trained minds will confront you with disturbing questions. "Where must one go out into space before he is likely to glimpse the pearly gates and golden streets and many mansions of the Sweet Bye and Bye?" Or about Jesus: "If He had to keep going up, up, up like an escaped balloon in order to get back to where He came from, please define for people like us who know ourselves to be dwellers on a spinning planet, in a wheeling solar system, part of a spiraling galaxie, tucked into a fold of an infinitely vast, shapeless universe — *just where is up?*"

The New Testament writers, however, though they themselves may have imagined the earth to be flat and the sky not far away, do not embarrass us with naive scientific blunders. They do not present heaven as a floating landscape above the stars. Instead, they talk about it as if it were a fifth dimension, although they do not use that terminology. They are describing life on another wave-length, although electronics was still an unlocked door. You would not faze them at all by informing them that "up" in Palestine is simultaneously "down" in the South Pacific, or that "up" at noon is "down" at midnight. Heaven for them, instinctively, is "where God is," whenever His presence is realized and His sovereignty acknowledged. We shall have fully entered heaven when we come to complete consciousness of that presence, plus the possession of resurrection bodies able to express the full devotion of our saved souls.

Read in Ephesians, for instance, what Paul has to say about "the heavenlies," as the King James Version translates the Greek. One senses that he is alluding to an unseen, eternal world which exists side by side with, and interpenetrates the whole of, space. If our mortal bodies were not so limited, we might reach out any time and touch this dimension of existence, just as we might at this moment tune in on scores of radio programs if our bodies had built-in receiving sets. No radical adjustment of our thinking process is required to turn from what the New Testament says in this connection to what modern physicists are discussing. The lovely line from naturalist John Muir's writings accords well with Paul:

"Around all the earth deep Heaven lies, and is a part of it."

With such analogies in mind we may begin to see how Jesus' ascension to the Father is just a stepping across the borderline from the seen to the unseen realm, from space-time into eternity. He could do it now, for He had inherited a new and perfectly responsive "spiritual body," to use Paul's language once again. And conversely, He can step back any time He wills to do so, out of eternity and back into space-time. He did just that for the conversion of the great Apostle and, according to some interesting testimony, has done so upon occasion for the benefit of others too.

More needful for us now than listing case histories is our grasping of the basic concept. Jesus is near! He is literally at hand, not merely to be invoked by one's imagination. But let us allow one witness to speak. He is F. Herbert Stead reporting in his book, *The Unseen Fellowship:*

> "One morning I had finished reading Keim's *Life of Jesus of Nazara.* His account of the resurrection filled me with a whirl of contending thoughts. His negative conclusions often aroused vigorous revulsion: his concessions to positive faith seemed to demand more.
>
> "I could not remain indoors. I set out at a brisk pace along Iffley Road towards the town. I came under the trees that leaned over the footway not far from Magdalen Bridge.
>
> "And then — O moment, one and infinite!
>
> "He was there beside me. No vision, nothing visible. No sound, nothing audible. No reminiscence, no phantasm, but Himself, Jesus once of Nazareth, unmistakably, overpoweringly He!
>
> "The certainty of sense, the certainty of mathematical proof, the certainty of conscience, were as nothing to the certainty of His self-revelation. The puny outposts of rationalism and subjectivism with their shrill demands for permits signed by the intellect, were all swept away as the King rode into the citadel of the soul. . . .
>
> "He gave me no message, He gave me no mandate. He did infinitely more. He made me to know Him to be the Present Companion, the Living Leader, the overmastering Lover.
>
> "Words fall like rotten rungs beneath the feet as one tries to climb toward the merest suggestion of what must remain forever ineffable. My whole being was one passionate vibration of awe, wonder, gratitude, love and adoration. I was as far removed as possible from being in any merely passive

state. It took all of me, every power within me raised to its
intensest activity to receive what I could of the infinite gift.
So I reached the very transport of certainty."

We are given to understand, whether or not we are as
vividly conscious of it as this man was permitted to be,
that Jesus is near. He ascended into heaven, not escalator
fashion, but stepping from one state of existence into
another. He would not have needed to "step." The cloud
was present only as an object lesson. It reiterated what
He had said a little earlier about being with them always.

If we wish to know our part of the arrangement, we do
well to turn to John's Gospel and to give close attention
to the passages which introduce the Holy Spirit, who
would soon be taking up His residence in the church as
Jesus' *alter ego*. God, you see, *is* Spirit. Those who seek
Him do not need to pilgrimage to sacred spots but only to
worship Him in spirit and in truth. Then whatever place
we stand is holy ground. Another incident:

> "Two men once met on a corner at a noisy city intersection.
> Both were haggard with fatigue. Each had heavy business
> responsibilities and the day had been hectic. They talked
> of various matters, including Church, for both were Christians.
> All at once the face of the one was seen to relax as if he
> were just back from a vacation, rested and ready for the job.
> The other could not conceal his surprise, and entering into
> the spirit of the moment asked, "Where in the world have
> you been?" The first replied, "I've been to the greatest verse
> in the Bible!" "Meaning? . . . ." And so he quoted: "Come
> unto me, all ye that labor and are heavy laden, and I will give
> you rest," and on to the end of that truly great, if not the
> greatest, word of Jesus."

Often it is by such a still, small voice that Jesus makes
himself known. The Holy Spirit operates like this in the
lives of countless Christians. And He can in yours!

If we learn to take Christ's nearness seriously, our personal lives will be quite changed, as will also be our public

worship. There is a special closeness to Him when we are in Christian company. The Lord's Supper is for many of us a peculiarly meaningful reminder of this fact. It is more than a ritual; it is a reunion. To us, as to the first disciples, He is saying, "Gather yourselves and make ready the table, and I shall be there as your Guest — and as your Host as well." So we continue to obey, recognizing His presence not as with the Roman Church in priestly performance of a substantial miracle, but because of our awareness that "Heaven lies about us" who are God's children. The words which He has spoken to us are Spirit. They are our Life. Indeed, whether a priest or minister is in sight or not has little importance except to prepare us for the sacrament by the preaching of the Word. The closeness of our Savior at the communion service or in any other act of Christian worship, just as much as in the lonely moments of our lives, is not by benefit of clergy! Neither is it the product of our own disciplined devotion. It is the result of a Divine arrangement which Jesus epitomized by stepping into the cloud. "I and the Father are One," He was saying, "and we will be with you until the end of time — nearer than breathing, closer than hands or feet."

Yet, this is only one side of the whole story concerning His whereabouts for concurrently:

2. We Are to Be Conscious of Jesus' Exaltation

Our Bible was composed at a time when men naturally thought of government in terms of monarchy. The clearest way to suggest God's authority and power was to picture Him as King.

This royal manner of speaking carried with it appropriate mental images. One naturally envisioned a cosmic court, with God seated upon a throne, high and lifted

up, surrounded by His servants and messengers to whom
He would give orders at will. John Milton, no longer able
to read but with his mind full of Scripture imagery, has
such a Sovereign in view:

> "   — — — — His state
> Is Kingly. Thousands at his bidding speed
> And post o'er Land and Ocean without rest:
> They also serve who only stand and wait."

No one makes sport of Milton's sonnet. If a modern
skeptic feels like poking fun at the oriental imagery our
Bible employs, there is plenty of it to entertain him. But
he is mistaken if he infers that whenever we proclaim
the sovereignty of God or give Him the title "King," we
are limiting Him to some throne room in the sky. No one
accuses the weather man of medieval metaphysics when
he reports the sun as due to "rise" at six A.M. tomorrow.
To speak of sunrise or of sunset is the figurative use of
language, as any sensible person recognizes right away.

So is that portion of the Creed which describes Jesus
Christ as ascended "to the right hand of God the Father
Almighty." There is no need to argue for a second throne
in prescribed position. The figure of speech has to do not
with location but with the exercise of power in the affairs
of men and in the universe at large. "All power is given
unto me, in Heaven and on earth," the risen Christ announced. The Greek work for power means "authority,"
too. He was, says Scripture, "declared to be the Son of
God with power by the resurrection from the dead."

A dear old lady now long dead was greatly troubled
when from the pulpit she was told not to think of God
as an old, old man with long white beard enthroned above
the clouds. She said that she simply could not picture Him
any other way. All right! Let Michelangelo's great paint-
ings serve their purpose for those who must conceive

of God in a literal palace on an actual throne or Jesus seated by His side. Just do not insist that the Bible requires something of the sort. We have no reason whatever to apologize to the mind of modern man when we rise to sing:

> "All hail the power of Jesus' name; let angels prostrate fall.
> Bring forth the royal diadem, and crown Him, Lord of all!"

What strikes me as being far more relevant, if one is looking for loopholes in Christian theology, is the question raised in almost anyone's mind by the last three words of the hymn just quoted. "Jesus Christ, the Lord of all? Why doesn't He act more like it? In our kind of a world with its rampant evil, its cruel injustices, its hunger-swollen bellies, its wars and waste and weariness of life, *Where is He?*"

The Bible does not dodge such questions. In fact, the whole Bible may be said to be about the very problem which this question pulls into focus. What the Old Testament illustrates in its account of the dealings of God with His B.C. people, the New Testament underlines with its saga of the Messiah: born in Bethlehem, hidden in Nazareth, teaching in Galilee, executed in Judea, rising gloriously from Joseph's garden tomb, stepping into the waiting cloud . . . and someday coming again, "in like manner as ye have seen him go." So the narrative of Jesus ends. And then the era of the church begins. The earth spins on. Worldly kingdoms wax and wane, and so does the vigor of the church; but while they perish and are forgotten, it sometimes flickers and sometimes flares but cannot be put out. This, too, is the power of Christ at work.

We live between the Times. Jesus came once to suffer and die. He shall come again to "judge the quick and the dead." The implication of that quaint but awe-full set

of words is that Christ's return with unveiled authority
will occur while civilization is in full swing.

Jesus' own explicit teaching tells us the same. We are
not to imagine ruefully that He is stymied by man's unbelief. He is not, as well intentioned preachers occasionally
try to tell us, tremulo stops pulled out to motivate us
more — He is not looking over Heaven's parapet and
wringing His hands because we are not more help. No,
this is the era during which by deliberate choice He leaves
the world to the tender mercies of the church. And the
church during this same period He has consigned to the
gentle, unobtrusive administration of the Holy Spirit. And
the Holy Spirit refuses to force issues. Virtue must be
voluntary to be virtue. Belief must be a calculated risk
to be true faith. Men must choose, first, whether to be
saved, and afterward, whether they will be good stewards.
All this is the strategy God uses precisely *because* Christ
is Lord of all. ("If He is not Lord of all," one has said,
"He is not Lord at all!") He is patient beyond human comprehension,

> ". . . not willing that any should perish, but that all should
> come to repentance."

The Second Epistle of Peter continues what we have
begun to quote:

> "But the day of the Lord will come as a thief in the night; in
> the which the heavens shall pass away with a great noise, and
> the elements shall melt with a fervent heat, the earth also and
> the works that are therein shall be burned up."

In the light of what we know about nuclear energy and
the "H" Bomb, some Bible interpreters apply this passage
very literally. One matter ought to be kept clear. Man will
not destroy himself with his atomic weapons. Conceivably he could, as apprehensive men of science warn. But

the Word of God disarms rebellious man of his panic button, just as it delivers His obedient children from the panic itself. Jesus Christ, who in His authority *is* the right hand of God, controls the outcome. In the fulness of time He came once, and in the fulness of time (the word suggests a pregnancy complete; about to issue in a birth) He will "descend from heaven with a shout," the Bible says. That shout will be a shout of undisputable victory.

I have tried to reflect the Biblical answer to the question: "Where is He?" The Bible itself gives its answer ever so much more eloquently and convincingly. When I hear a Christian complaining about the apparent impotence of the Lord while the wicked flourish and the innocent groan, I know he hasn't been reading his Bible much lately. Myself included!

For us who love Him it is given to know that God is working in all events for good. To us who will trust Him, our Christ draws back the curtain and in His Word reveals what history has in store. "God who commanded the light to shine out of darkness (in creation) has shined in our hearts, to give the light of the knowledge of his glory (read "majesty," if you wish) in the face (that is, the total portrait we have of Him in the New Testament) of Jesus Christ."

When Jesus stepped into the cloud, a little less than six weeks after He had risen from the dead, he was assuming once again the majesty of Deity. We are to cultivate a continuing consciousness, from the Word of God with the help of the Holy Spirit, of His exaltation.

The benefits from such a consciousness, in terms of courage, durable joy and efficient Christian performance, could be illustrated from the lives of many famous Christians, beginning with the apostles, whose preaching echoed with it, or with Stephen, who died triumphantly under a rain of cobblestones affirming that he saw Jesus standing on the right hand of God, waiting to welcome him Home.

What could satisfy me more than other illustrations would be the kind of evidence in my own life, and in yours, arising from firsthand experience of what the Lord promised before He left:

> "Verily, verily I say unto you. He that believeth on me, the works that I do shall he do also; and greater works than these shall he do; *because I go unto my Father.* And whatsoever ye shall ask in my name, that will I do, that the Father may be glorified in the Son" (John 14:12, 13).

I like the choice Jesus made when it came time for Him to go. I am glad He decided to preach His final sermon by stepping into the radiant cloud. It would be plain to those who saw Him go, as well as to countless others after who might read about it. It emphasized His nearness and His exaltation, His immanence and His transcendence. And these twin truths can make a glorious difference in a Christian's life.

I trust they have made a difference in our life together in this church today. We are not remembering a lost leader. We have been enjoying a reunion with our living Lord and giving Him, I trust, the royal welcome He deserves.

Chapter X

Two Roads to Christian Certitude

"Jesus said to him, 'Have you believed because you have seen me? Blessed are those who have not seen and yet believe.'" — John 20:29

Jesus sounds at first as if he were implying that it is a sin to be scientific, and that ignorance is bliss.

If this is what His words to Thomas mean, then some of us, sadly perhaps but resolutely, will have to turn our backs on the church. "To thine own self be true!" says the poet. And for a person who has been born with an inquiring mind, any attempt, even in the name of religion, to smother that native curiosity will set up an irreconcilable conflict. Just as one would have to repudiate any interpretation of Christianity which might propose some violation of one's basic code of ethics, so it would be an affront to a man's intellectual integrity if a condition of being a Christian were the choking off of all questions.

Fortunately, Jesus is saying no such thing. Implicit in His dealing with His doubt-riddled disciple is a very real sympathy for his problem. His tenderness with Thomas comforts me no end. Apparently the proverbial "Man from Missouri" with his "show me" approach can still be a Christian!

But then Jesus goes one step further and makes clear that in times to come others will be coming to Christian faith in general, and to certitude concerning His resurrection in particular, by another less painful route than that which Thomas has taken. Here is good news, too!

One summer when I was a boy I went with two friends on a hike up what we supposed to be one of the loneliest and least accessible mountains in central New Hampshire. We struggled for most of one day through the swamps and tangled thicket at its base, and then on up its increasingly sheer sides until in the late afternoon we made the summit and prepared to set up camp. We had the feeling of lonely achievement which only true pioneers can know! Imagine the shock when an hour or two before sunset, we heard the sound of a mixed quartet in cheerful conversation. A party of city-folks had sauntered up a lumberman's road from the other side and were going to see the view and get back to their car in plenty of time before dark! Naturally we were annoyed by the casual arrival of that bunch of tenderfeet, but in retrospect we had to admit that the mountain did not belong to us. We had had our rugged climb. No need to begrudge them their easier one.

There are two corresponding ways of arriving at Christian certitude. One is,

1. *The Trail of Scientific Evidence*

Thomas needed evidence before he could believe.

"Doubting Thomas" we call him, and the nickname has a way of triggering two quite different trains of thought.

Some favored folk, who have never had much difficulty believing, find it easy to diagnose Thomas as a case of stubborn sinfulness. Instead of acquiescing in the joy that had broken over the other disciples when they saw the Lord, he seemed to want to talk them out of their assurance. I have observed that sort of malignant skepticism at work, and it is not a pretty thing. There are unbelievers who take an evil delight in sowing seeds of doubt in fertile young minds, and in watching the consequent crop of thorns and thistles grow to choke out the good seeds planted in church and Sunday school. A college teacher of philosophy was discussing a freshmen who had come to school full of Christian zeal. "We have got to save that fellow's soul!" said the professor, which translated meant the launching of an attack on his "eccentricity" and reducing his enthusiasm to ashes. Collegians, at least in that institution, were not supposed to take traditional Christianity seriously. And I am sorry to report that the assault on that particular freshman's faith succeeded, at least in the years I knew him.

Jesus had some strong words to characterize those who put stumbling blocks to belief in the way of the young. It would be better for such peddlers of apostasy, He indicated, for them to be thrown, millstone around neck, into the depths of the sea! Was Thomas that kind of a character?

For others he is not a sinister type at all, but rather patron saint of the honest, anguished intellectual of whom the literary world is so proud these days. Men like Camus and Sartre, like Bertrand Russell and the best selling Bishop of Woolwich, for all their variety of stance and style, are telling us how terribly hard it is for the

brain to believe. Dear dubious Thomas talks their language and sanctifies their despair.

The truth about him probably lies somewhere between
these two extremes. He is neither to be damned nor praised
for his unhappiness. It may have been mostly temperamental: determined by the way his genes fell together
and how his glands functioned and by the electrical
circuits (or short-circuits) in his grey matter. People do
differ in these respects, you know. If Thomas were rein-
carnated as a modern schoolboy, he might well get good
marks in math and chemistry but be mediocre in English
and Art. No! That isn't quite fair, because what we are
talking about goes deeper than a person's intellectual
aptitudes. It has more to do with attitudes. Some people
have a basically scientific feeling for life, others a more
poetic one. (One may have the former and still flunk
chemistry, or the latter and not do well in English composition!) What we mean is that the poetic temperament
moves a man to arrive at truth most naturally by the
faculty called intuition. He learns by a kind of osmosis.
The scientific frame of mind calls on the other hand for
a process of testing and classifying. It compels a man to
deal with a problem in philosophy or theology like a
trained mechanic who is about to buy himself an auto-
mobile.

Admittedly no one is pure scientist or absolute poet.
Yet most of us "lean" one way or the other, just as we
habitually fold our hands with either the left thumb
or the right thumb consistently on top! We may suppose
that Thomas was a tester by temperament.

Jesus' words to Thomas, which serve as our text, are
usually taken as a rebuke. We need not deny that there
was an element of criticism in what was said. Every man
is a sinner, and he was no exception. Like us, he may have

let his natural temperament serve him as an excuse for being more "difficult" than he needed to be. "Except this and except that," he growled, "I *will* not believe." That is like pushing out one's lower lip and saying to God, "You made me the way I am. Change me if you can!" And all of us have talked this way at times. Furthermore, without intending to be rude he was in effect calling his fellow disciples liars, or at least fools. After three years of companionship with them, he might have credited them with some sense and with a measure of wholesome skepticism of their own! How easy it is to conclude that when we are out of step with the rest of the marchers, they are the ones who are uncoordinated! Thomas was revealing a certain lack of humility in his insistence upon being shown, and Jesus' mild rebuke was in order.

But I prefer to see, as predominating in Jesus' words to him, not so much rebuke as reassurance. The intent is not to shame but to comfort him. We may paraphrase it this way:

> "Thomas, you said you wanted evidence. Is that true? Are you really openminded? If so, there is evidence for you, and I'm glad to give you just as much as you will need. Here, touch the nail prints. If your stomach can stand it, thrust your hand into the spear hole in my side. Don't wallow in your doubts. Take my hand and clamber out of them. There is certitude for you and for any other compulsive truth-tester who loves me, as I know you do!"

We are not told whether Thomas fully followed through with the opportunity for investigation which Jesus offered. That his inquiring mind was satisfied is apparent. "Lord," he was saying with tears, "Lord, I believe!"

Thomas represents the fact that for those whose mental make up demands it, adequate evidence for the existence of God, the trustworthiness of the Bible, and the reality of Christ's resurrection is available. But we must recognize that while God welcomes the honestly critical approach whether in biology or theology or in any other branch of learning, He does not yield to the impertinent probings of vain men who worship their own minds. He sends His sun and rain upon His rebellious sons as well as on the loyal. He opens His treasure store of material goods to his faithful stewards as well as to those whose aim is to exploit and enslave their fellows. "Know how" is not the private property of the saints, nor of nominally Christian countries either. The fact that we engrave "In God We Trust" on our pennies did not prevent Sputnik from getting aloft first, and many other times an unbelieving man or nation has led the way into some new discovery of truth. Nevertheless, says Scripture, there is an essential wisdom which no amount of cleverness or sweat will enable us to attain unless we have a willingness to be taught by and responsible to the One who invented our minds. Reverence is the healthy scientific attitude. What the Bible calls unbelief is a sickness. No amount of evidence will satisfy it any more than a score of medical examinations will convince the hypochondriac that he is not dying of cancer or hopelessly infested with a myriad of lethal germs.

Thomas' problem may have been temperamental, but he was a man of good will, and therefore Jesus could deal helpfully with his doubt.

The principles we have been discussing apply specifically to the trouble some of us have with the resurrection story. There is no dodging the fact, disturbing to many, that in announcing that resurrection the New Testament witnesses are claiming His literal, bodily rising from the dead. Paul testifies pointedly that if that is not what happened, the Christian church might as well close up shop and go home. "But," he says in effect, "it *is* true, and there is adequate evidence to convince even an old skeptic like me!"

"Yes," says someone, turning from the Bible page, "there was evidence enough for Paul and for Peter, for James and John and Mary, Jesus' mother, and at last for Thomas, too. But is there enough to meet the need of a Twentieth Century inquirer?" Well, listen to this from one of the great scholars of modern times:

> "Indeed, taking all the evidence together, it is not too much to say that there is no single historic incident better or more variously supported than the resurrection of Christ. Nothing but the antecedent assumption that it must be false could have suggested the idea of deficiency in the proof of it."
> — Canon B. F. Westcott, *The Gospel of the Resurrection,* 4th Ed., pp. 4-6

Does that sound excessive? What he means, I think, is that according to the commonly accepted laws of evidence, and using the criteria of courts of law and of students of historical records, Jesus' resurrection is the only satisfactory explanation of, for example, the existence of this church, this Bible, and this act of Easter worship in which we share.

As I have mentioned before, there is considerable technical literature to support the Westcott statement. And there are some very helpful popular summaries for those of us who are more at home with the Readers Digest than with Karl Barth's Dogmatics! I am personally convinced that any earnest questioner can, if he will, satisfy himself in this matter. It is my conviction, further, that God made some of us with minds which cannot be satisfied except as we climb the painful trail to certitude through a step-by-step sifting of the evidence. If such is the predestined path for you or me, we need not complain. It can be an adventure, as exciting in its own right as the search for buried treasure, or as conquering a mountain the hard way. Which brings us to consider, secondly:

II. *The Pathway of Personal Experience*

"The Heart has its reasons," wrote Blaise Pascal, "that the Reason cannot know." You have heard the quotation before? I do not hesitate to repeat it because it is in my judgment the best, most concise statement to be found anywhere in justification of what we are calling the pathway of personal experience. Or perhaps one should say that it is the best statement to this effect found anywhere outside of the Word of God itself.

One reason why Pascal's sentence carries such weight is because he happened to be one of the greatest men of science who ever lived. He had the intellect of a genius, but he was also, after his conversion, a man of spiritual perceptiveness who understood the truth of Jesus' statement to Thomas: "Blessed are they that have not seen and yet have believed."

Pascal's respect for the reasons of the heart had its source in his own conversion experience — a fascinating story derived from the discovery of a piece of parchment sewed into the lining of his clothing and not found until after he had died. It represented a series of notes, scribbled first on a scrap of paper, in which this man, always the painstaking observer, took down his impressions of what God was saying to him while He was saving him. The date is carefully noted, and how he felt, and what he sensed and heard. Some of the text is Scripture, and some is his own attempt to express the inexpressible; a joy unspeakable and full of glory. Then comes this passage:

> "God of Abraham! God of Isaac! God of Jacob!
> Not of the philosophers and scholars.

> God of Jesus Christ!
> Thy God shall be my God."

and the conclusion:

> "He is to be found only in the ways taught in the Gospel."

The man of science had learned first hand that there is another way of being sure than by the weighing of evidence. God knows how to make Himself known immediately to the heart of the one who truly seeks Him.

The Apostle Paul, too, graduated one day from being a critic to a convert. He too had an analytical mind, and was trained in the best scholarship of his day. It was God's mercy, he confessed ever afterward, that had broken in upon his laborious process of rationalization; it was Jesus the Christ who had given him shock treatment which broke up the rigid, repetitious patterns of his prejudices and allowed him a glimpse of His resurrection glory. Paul did not cease being a scholar, but his preaching (which like all of the preaching of the early church centered in the resurrection message) was not lecturing but proclamation. There is a difference between the two. The lecturer sets out to demonstrate a thesis by the systematic presentation of evidence. Paul knew how to lecture with the best of them in Athens and in Corinth, and in Ephesus where he disputed daily in the school of Tyrranus for two whole years. But he had discovered that what might require as much as two years of patient lecturing to win the intellectual assent of philosophers, could be communicated almost instantaneously and just as conclusively in a single sermon to all classes of hearers. When by a deep heart instinct a man is ready to confess that Jesus of Nazareth deserves the place of Lord in his life; when his hunger and thirst for righteousness gets a fair taste of what Jesus has to offer; then not infrequently by one great leap of comprehension he will recognize with a wisdom too profound for words that the Resurrection gospel must be true. Is this not what Paul is meaning when he writes:

> "Say not in thine heart, Who shall ascend into heaven? (that is, to bring Christ down from above:) or, Who shall descend into the deep? (that is to bring up Christ again from the dead.) But what saith it? The word is nigh thee, even in thy mouth, and in thine heart: that is, the word of faith, which we preach. That if thou shalt confess with thy mouth the Lord Jesus, and shalt believe in thine heart that God hath raised Him from the dead, thou shalt be saved. For *with the heart* man believeth unto righteousness . . ." (Romans 10:6-10).

What we are urging here, on the basis of Jesus' second word to Thomas, is that the way of personal experience, rightly understood, is just as legitimate as the way of scientific investigation in arriving at God's truth. And this applies to belief in Christ's resurrection in particular. The explorations of the mind and the experiences of the soul are not exclusive of one another, or in any sense contradictory, although they may become strangers if too rigidly kept apart. But they can be honorably reconciled and, as God intended, can wholesomely supplement and reinforce each other.

The relationship between the Christian's head and heart in his search for truth remind me somewhat of the relationship between what in logic are called inductive and deductive reasoning. Inductive reasoning travels from particular facts to a general conclusion.

> Dr. Carvewell has examined thousands of damaged livers of heavy drinkers and concludes that there is a definite correlation between alcoholism and cirrhosis.

That is inductive reasoning. Deductive reasoning travels from an accepted principle to a specific application.

> Dr. Peering, who has read widely in the studies of Carvewell

and others, says to Joe Smith who has hepatitis, "Don't you
dare touch alcohol. It is dangerous for sick livers."

These are two approaches to truth and they work nicely
together.

If Thomas is to be identified as primarily an inductive
thinker who must have the facts all in before he is about
to come to a conclusion, whom shall we find to illustrate
the deductive approach where the heart soars ahead and
beckons for the mind to follow?

Paul would type well, as we have noticed, for the role.
I am not sure that any one of the eleven would really suit,
at least not until a little later. Perhaps we have too easily
assumed that Thomas was the only skeptic among them
and that Jesus singles him out for special attention on that
account. "Look at Peter and Andrew! Look at Nathaniel
and Philip! You don't see them dragging their feet, do
you? Buck up, Thomas, and get with it!"

So? When we read the whole story from beginning to
end, we may be ready to conclude that the disciples are
actually telling the Thomas incident as a reflection on
themselves. That usually is the spirit of the Gospel writers.
Read the resurrection narratives again and see whether
you do not agree. Just as Peter had often earlier spoken
for the entire company, as when he confessed Jesus' Mes-
siahship, or balked at the prediction of the cross, or
blatantly denied his discipleship, so Thomas can be said
to symbolize the last-ditch doubt of the whole crowd of
them.

He expresses their corporate confession. Reading between the lines, we hear them say, "Thomas stood for all
of us after the resurrection. We all were full of doubts.
Good old Thomas got the spotlight that evening, and the
label 'doubter' stuck to him. Of course, he had his problems with his doubts, but so did we. A week or so before,

when Jesus came into the room where we were gathered, we were terrified and thought He was a ghost. He had to rebuke us for our hardness of heart. We had spent so many of the precious moments in Galilee, and on the way to Jerusalem, and in the Upper Room, squabbling about who would have the best seats in the Kingdom that we hadn't really listened when He foretold His murder and His rising from the tomb. We were, if anything, *more* crushed, *more* utterly disillusioned than Thomas on that terrible crucifixion weekend. He was a natural born pessimist who generally expected the worst so as not to be surprised by tragedy. We weren't one bit more 'spiritual' than he! But that was long ago, and we were long ago forgiven!"

There is no reason to idealize any of the disciples or to imagine that since they had known Jesus in the flesh, faith in His resurrection came automatically for them.

Consequently, I am inclined to believe that the contrast drawn in Jesus' words to Thomas was not calculated to distinguish him from the others present, or them from him. It deals with two types of temperament, on the surface of it, as we have observed. But more profoundly it takes into account two sorts of situation. The time would come, as He had warned them earlier, when none of them would any longer see Him with the physical eye. Circumstances would arise in which there would be no chance for leisurely investigation or scholarly discussions pro and con. They would be dragged into court, or into the arena, and forced to deny their Lord or die. Thomas and all the others would soon learn that certitude at times must come like Stephens' vision, as a flash of insight, at the crucial moment, with complete authority.

The obedient heart as well as the investigative mind has its reasons!

We are the heirs of the same great truth. There is in the beatitude of our text ("blessed are they that have not seen and yet have believed!") an echo of the conversation which John records in his Chapters 14 through 16 and of the great High Priestly prayer which follows in the seventeenth chapter:

> "Neither pray I for these alone [i.e., Thomas and the other ten] but *for them also which shall believe on me through their word* . . . that they all may be one; as thou Father art in me, and I in thee, that they also may be one in us; that the world may believe that thou hast sent me."

Here, as eleven days afterward when He dealt with Thomas' doubt, the Lord evidently has in view a whole new class of disciples. They are the great multitude which no man can number, who shall come into being after Jesus has gone Home to the Father, and after the Holy Spirit has come to organize and to inhabit the church.

He is arranging by means of this prayer to give His people the second road to certitude. It had been occasional before, but now it would be by the Holy Spirit within them, instantly accessible whenever they needed it. Before long Paul would be writing about it to his friends in Rome. Do you remember?

> "The word is nigh thee, in thy mouth and in thine heart — that is, the word of faith which we preach."

In our congregation we are not as familiar as some with what are called "gospel songs." We criticize them because they tend to employ easy music which is not always structurally good, and some of them popularize a rather weak theology. But there are exceptions, and many gospel songs can teach us truths we need to learn and hold. Take for instance the one which has this for its chorus:

"He lives! He lives! Christ Jesus lives today!
He walks with me, and talks with me
And guides me on life's way.
He lives! He lives! salvation to impart.
You ask me how I know He lives?
He lives within my heart."

That is a song of the personal experience pathway to Christian certitude.

Most ministers have been exposed in their student days to a host of anecdotes from the lives of famous predecessors. Of these stories, one oft-repeated comes from the life of R. W. Dale who for many years occupied the pulpit of the Carrs Lane Congregational Church in Birmingham, England. Dr. Dale was a world renowned preacher, a theologian, and an effective social reformer. One day in his study while working on his Sunday message, quite suddenly and without warning he was struck almost as with a physical impact by the meaning of Jesus' resurrection. Leaping to his feet, he paced the floor, repeating aloud to himself with a kind of awe: "Jesus Christ is alive. He is alive!" What had occurred? He had not turned up any new facts, but he had arrived at a wonderful new comprehension that to believe Christ risen is more than to credit a fact of history. It means to discover Him as the living Lord and Companion of one's life.

Dr. Dale testifies that his ministry was transformed and that from that day it had a new dimension. Something similar, though specifically suited to you, awaits you whenever, to the reasons of the head, you will offer the full response of your heart.

We may labor up the steep slopes of scientific inquiry, or make our way along the less painstaking road of personal experience. Each of us is called to direct his steps toward the goal for the prize of the upward call in Christ Jesus.

Paul had in view a footrace when he used these familiar phrases in his Philippian letter. It could just as well have been a mountain climb. His Christian goal was identical with ours, and he describes it in words which make a superb Easter motto:

> "That I may know him, and the power of his resurrection, and the fellowship of his sufferings, being made conformable unto his death; if by any means [by whatever road I travel] I might attain unto the resurrection from the dead."

Whichever of these two roads *you* prefer to travel (they intersect occasionally and one may follow either, or both, from time to time) may *evidence* and *experience* bring you soon to Christian certitude!